The Golden Sun Egg Uncracked
The Spiritual Meaning of Neggur
Dr Nteri Nelson

Synopsis
Secrets of Race & Consciousness
Afrikan Comogenesis & Cosmology of Kemet

The Golden Sun Egg Uncracked
The NU'N' Word Negg ur The Goose God/dess Who Laid The Sun Egg, the Cosmic Egg

The Wsir/Ausarianization of Consciousness
Tablet Series 2 – A.C.T.S. 3

Dr. Terri Nelson
Nteri Renenet Elson

**Afrikan Cosmogenesis & Cosmology of Kemet
The Nu 'N' Word**

This work is a synopsis, derivative and clarifying of an earlier and more comprehensive work of the same Title.
Copyright © 2000, 2003, 2005, 2008, 2009, 2022 Dr Terri Nelson. Library of Congress Cataloging in Publication

The press of Spirit causes this work to go forward now even though it is still undergoing editing phases.

Data
All Rights Reserved. No part of this book maybe used or reproduced in any manner whatsoever without written permission except in the case of brief quotations embodied in critical articles and reviews. All inquiries may be forwarded to the address below.

ISBN: 978-0-9659600-0-7
Printed in the United States of America

Published by: The Academy of Kemetic Education, Right Relationship Maat, Inc.
53 Cedar St.
Mattapan, MA 02126

The Golden Sun Egg Uncracked
The Spiritual Meaning of Neggur
Dr Nteri Nelson

The author is available for group lectures and individual consultations. For further information or to order additional copies contact:
АЖЕ

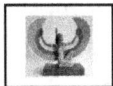 

**The AЖademy of Kemetic Education, Inc.
Right Relationship and Right Knowledge**

African Origin of The Ancient/Egyptian Wisdom
Awakening Жonsciousness
AfriKan Жnowledge
Wsir/Ausarian Enlightenment
The Knowledge & Education That Awakens 1st Eye Awareness into
The Metaphysics, Art & Science of Daily Living
*Leading to Spiritual Transformation, Right Relationship,
Soul Purpose Living, & Service*
Classes Held at: 53 Cedar St., Mattapan, MA 02126
www.rrrk.net   (617) 296 - 7797

About The Author
Terri Nelson, PhD.E, L.I.C.S.W., M.S.W., M.S.E.P., Shækem RA АЖЕ (Reiki) Master
aka Nteri Renenet Elson
The Netcherw revealing Harvest to the Sons and Daughters of God

Dr. Nteri Nelson is a Metaphysician, Licensed Clinician, Priestess of Kemet and Teacher of the Afrikan origins of the Ancient wisdom. She is co-founder of, *The Academy of Kemetic Education, Right Relationship Right Knowledge, Maat, Inc.* where she teaches an Afrikan Centered Model for Psychological, Spiritual, and Character development which is underpinned by the History of Ancient Afrika/Kemet (Egypt) and the Diaspora as a way of Self knowledge, healing and health. Her classes on the application of the Ancient Wisdom in Modern Daily Living are helping others find solutions to life challenges. A specialty area which she brings penetrative insight to is, *The Spiritual and Psychological Journey of Unfolding Consciousness out of Afrika.* Dr. Nteri is a gifted Wordsmith and Medew Netcher Symbologist and has given important Keys for Dis-Spelling Illusion in her books.

She has a Bachelor of Science in Psychology (B.S); a Masters in Social Work (M.S.W); a Masters in the Science of Esoteric Psychology (M.S.E.P); and a Doctor of Esoteric Philosophy (PhD.E) with a concentration in Metaphysical and Kemetic Egyptian Studies. She is an Independent researcher of the Ancient Wisdom teachings and was a member of The Black Knostic Study Group for several years under the late Dr. Alfred Ligon. She has had the honor of traveling to Kemet (Egypt) under the guidance of Elder Dr. Yosef ben Jochannan and Dr. Clinton Crawford; and to Ghana under the guidance of Drs. Leonard and Rosalind Jeffries and Professor James Small. As teacher and eternal student of the Ancient wisdom her years of experience have made her a firsthand witness to that which both fetters and liberates the Soul in its Spiritual Journey. She has been garnering and distributing the wisdom and tools for Wsir/Ausarian Spiritual Transformation and Resurrection or ASTR (STAR).

She has worked in the behavioral/mental health field for the last 35 years and her training has included both traditional and alternative approaches to healing. She has had a private practice where she uses a variety of healing methods. She provides counseling and consultation to: individuals, couples families, groups and agencies. Co-counseling together, she and her husband, Lester Nelson, Min., specialize in relationship work with couples, individuals, families and groups.

Dr Terri Nelson is author of: *Ka Ab Ba Building The Lighted Temple; Secrets of Race and Consciousness; On The Way To Finding Your Soulmate; The Right Relationship Workbook* and *The Forgiveness Process Workbook*. She has given lectures nationally and internationally which includes: the Association for the Study of Classical Afrikan Civilization (ASCAC); Indigenous Afrikan Healers Conference; First World Alliance in New York; Institute for the Study of Race and Culture; The Melanin Conference; Sankofa; Medew Netcher; etc.

This book is dedicated to –
•AMEN, Infinite Eternal All in All, Netcher Netcherw, Fount of All Possibility,
•*Father/Mother Creator, Most High God/Goddess in Whom we live and move and have our being, Divined as Wsir/AusarAuset,*
•*and to the Paut Netcherw, the company of the Gods, guiding us into sacred space, imbruing us*

6 Afrikan Cosmogenesis & Cosmology of Kemet
The Nu 'N' Word

with all God qualities (Netcherw), teaching us to live as Gods and Goddesses,
•and to the Ancestors who have gone before,
Those who have remained steady in the Light and
Those with hard won footsteps who have trodden their way back into the Light and
Those with heavy laden footsteps who are treading their way onto the path of Light
•In all praise and appreciation that you hear our prayers

Tree of Life Great Pyramid MerAkhutu

KaAbBa   MerKaBa
          Heru
Het-Heru   Sebek
  Maat   Auset   Herukhuti
     Nit   Khnemu
Tehuti   Seker
© Dr Terri Nelson
    ™   Ausar
           Geb
          AMEN
Paut Neteru, Solar Bark, Chariot of the Gods

The Golden Sun Egg Uncracked
The Spiritual Meaning of Neggur

Dr Nteri Nelson

African Cosmology, African Centered Education
The Psychological & Spiritual Journey
of Unfolding Consciousness
Metaphysics and Mysteries

Kemet (also spelled Kmt, Kamit) is the name of the land, of the Ancient Nile Valley Civilization, in Africa. The people who inhabited this land were called the Kemetians. This land and its people would later be re-named Egypt and Egyptians respectively, by the Greeks. These Kemites, our African Ancestors, used picture images or ideographs from nature all around them to communicate ideas, in the language they called Mdu Ntr. This is variously spelled as, Mtu Ntr, Mtw Ntr, Metu Neter, Medu Neter and Medew Netcher. This language and its symbols were later re-named Hieroglyphics, by the Greeks.

The power and vibe of words and symbols have become garbled and distorted as Medew Netcher made its journey into English. In our study of Afrikan Cosmology of Kemet, the Nu 'N' Word and the Spiritual meaning of name(s) **'Negg-ur' 'Negneg ur', 'Gengen ur'** is revealed. The Medew Netcher are the pictographs and letters which act as oracle to energetically convey the Netcherw or qualities of divinity. The Nu 'N' word, in contrast to the colonizing 'N' word, brings us into understanding a state of Unitive consciousness and wholeness, symbolized by the, **Golden Sun Egg Uncracked.**

The Nu 'N' Word

As an Afrikan people we are millions of years old. When we were with the Medew Netcher, the divine speech of the Gods, all that we built through the sounding of a 'word' reflected that divinity. The Kemetic Law of Vibration teaches that Words have a vibration. Words may vibrate at a higher Spiritual level, a more refined level. Likewise, words may vibrate at a lower, coarse, dense and material level. When Medew Netcher was vibrating at this higher Spiritual and refined level, this contributed to our greatness as an Afrikan people.

As we made our footsteps out of Afrika we populated the world. As such, Medew Netcher, *The WORD, words, speech, symbol and idea* have gone forth as a language that has journeyed out of Afrika also. As the Medew Netcher journeyed out of Afrika it became confused, garbled, and distorted by its distillation through the English language. As the Medew Netcher went out into English, - 'words' - were negatively potentized to contribute to our demise as a people. We began to experience fragmentation, separativeness, and brokenness in consciousness. Its resultant lower vibratory expression has contributed to the deep psychological pain we must heal so that we may return to the source of our Greatness.

As Afrikan and Afrikan Diaspora, the Nu 'N' word is the pathway to understanding the resurrection of ourselves from the devastating impact and concentrated pollutant of the colonizing 'N' word. As we ungarble the 'NU'N' Word and see the

The Golden Sun Egg Uncracked
The Spiritual Meaning of Neggur
Dr Nteri Nelson

probable distortion of an ancient harmonic, our footsteps re-trace a path deep within our Afrikan Cosmology and Cosmogenesis. We thereby reconnect ourselves (particularly our youth) to that which 'rings true' to Our Story, our healing and our Mother Afrika. Through this reconnection - the resurrection of the Medew Netcher, as inextricably linked with our own - is revealed, and will:

1) Reconnect (especially our youth) with Afrikan Cosmogenesis, Cosmology and History.
2) Stir revelation, deep thought, and resurrection out of the quagmire of confusion about words that have been used to describe, enslave, rob and kill the Black man and Black woman.
3) Reveal the Spiritual and Psychological Journey of Unfolding Consciousness, the Afrikan Cosmogenesis and Cosmology of Kemet, the Sacredness of the Cosmic Sun Egg, and differentiate Higher Spiritual meaning of the Nu'N' word from the colonizing 'N' word.
4) Retrace, ferret out and dispel word meaning.
5) Dissipate the power to wound that the N word(s) has had as the Medew Netcher have gone out into English.
6) Point the way toward healing so that we may return to the source of our greatness.
7) Wordsmith word meaning at both lower and higher spirals of vibration and dis-spell illusion so that we may reclaim and use

power at its most potent, optimal and divine Spiritual level of vibration.

This book is a Synopsis of earlier works. Like a mathematician, I included the calculations and permutations or 'scratch work' in these earlier volumes. This work extracts all of that out, gives the conclusions, putting them into a concise Book of readable pages. Rather than be repetitive throughout the text, I refer the reader here, just once, to the expanded information, diagrams, etc. which will be found in the full volumes of, **Ka Ab Ba Building The Lighted Temple** and **The Secrets of Race and Consciousness.** Please refer to these for supportive and background explanation, as well as penetrative focus on how to become skilled Kemeticians/Metaphysicians. Additionally, the words Neter and God are used interchangeably, not because of their exact correspondence, but in order to provide a bridge in consciousness for the reader.

The Golden Sun Egg Uncracked
The Spiritual Meaning of Neggur
Dr Nteri Nelson

African Cosmogenesis & Cosmology of Kemet
The Planetary Goose God 'Negg-ur' 'Negneg ur', 'Gengen ur' Who Laid the Golden Egg

According to the people of Kemet (later called Egypt by the Greeks) Geb was the God of Earth. Our purpose is to understand the meaning of the Planetary God Geb, (also pronounced, Keb and Seb). The God Geb is pictured at right. The goose was sacred to Geb and is seen on top of his head. Accordingly: E.A. Wallis Budge. *The Gods of the Egyptians, V.II*, p. 95-96.

> The goose was sacred to Geb and he was believed to have made his way through the air in its form. Geb was the god of the earth, and the earth formed his body and was called the "house of Geb".

He is also called, 'Negg ur', 'Negneg ur', 'Gengen ur', who laid the Golden Sun Egg. This is expressed according: E.A. Wallis Budge. *An Egyptian Hieroglyphic Dictionary*, p. 398,

Negg ur, Negneg ur – the Goose-goddess who laid the sun-egg. Vol. l, p. 398.

Gengen ur – the Goose-god who laid the Cosmic Egg, Vol. ll, p. 809.

Geb and his female counterpart Nut produce the great Egg. Geb, the erpat of the gods is called, "the Great Cackler". In the Kemetic tradition, the Divine Goose or "Great Cackler," laid the Cosmic Egg. This is expressed accordingly: E.A. Wallis Budge. *The Book of the Dead*, p.176:

> Originally he was the god of the earth, and is called both the "father of the gods", and the "*erpā* (*i.e.*, the tribal, hereditary head) of the gods." He is depicted in human form, sometimes with a crown upon his head and the sceptre in his right hand; and sometimes he has upon his head a goose, which bird was one of his incarnations. In many places he is called the "great cackler", and he was supposed to have laid the egg from which the world sprang. Already in the Pyramid Texts he has become a god of the dead by virtue of representing the earth wherein the deceased was laid.

▲ The Nu'N' Word
The Most Primal 'N' Word is Nu or Nun

What is Nu (Nun) and the arising of the Cosmic Egg? In understanding of Cosmogony and Cosmogenisis, the Creation of Universe, we understand that: Within the INFINITE, BOUNDLESS ALL, AMEN - there is a *Stirring*. Within this INFINITE, BOUNDLESS, BLACKNESS, DARKNESS OF SPIRIT, The ABSOLUTE ALL AND ALL *Stirs* within the limitless unconditioned substance of ITSELF. This Spirit/Matter is called – Nu or Nun, by the Kemetians.* It is the primeval waters, the

---

* See Budge, *Prt Em Hru. (The Egyptian Book of the Dead)*.

The Golden Sun Egg Uncracked
The Spiritual Meaning of Neggur
Dr Nteri Nelson

primordial, pre-stellar, pre-birthing substance, the waters of space.

Our Kemetic Story of Creation is retranslated and expressed accordingly: E.A. Wallis Budge, *The Gods of The Egyptians, V.I,* p. 313-321. (Papyrus of Nes-Amsu) "The Book of Knowing the Evolutions of Ra, and of Overthrowing Apepi," excerpts from Version A and B. Note: My insertions will be expressed in brackets as follows:{[ ]}.

This is expressed accordingly in Version A
>The words of Neb-er-tcher, {[the Neb/lord of the Universe and a form of the Sun – god Ra]}, [which] he spoke after he had come into being: I was the creator of what came into being. I am he who came into being in the form of Khepera, I was (or, became) the creator of what came into being, the creator of all what came into being, the creator of what came into being all; after my coming into being many [were] the things which came into being coming forth from my mouth…

This is expressed accordingly in Version B
>The words of Neb-er-tcher. He says: - I was (or, the creator of what came into being. I came into being in the forms of Khepera coming into being in primeval time. I came into being in the forms of Khepera. I was (or, became) the creator of what came into being, that is to say, I produced myself from the primeval matter [which] I made. I produced myself from primeval matter. My name

is Ausares the primeval matter of primeval matter...I brought [into] my mouth my own my name, that is to say, a word of power, and I, even I, came into being in the form of things which came into being, and I came into being in the forms of Khepera. I came into being from the primeval matter, coming into being [in] multitudes of forms from the beginning. Not existed any created things in this land; I made whatsoever was made everything.

I {[Ra]} was alone, not existed [any other] who worked with me in that place. I made (all) the forms therein by means (or, out of) the divine soul {[Ba, Cosmic Sun Egg, One Universal Ba, Periodical Universe, Eye of Ra, World Soul]} that [which] I raised up therein out of Nu (i.e., the primeval abyss of water) from a state inertness {[or inert mass]}.

Not found I {[there, i.e., in Nu) a place whereon I could stand. I worked with the Spirit {[Khut]} [which] was in my heart, I laid a foundation before me, I made all whatsoever {[that]} was made. I was alone, I laid a foundation in my heart, I made the other things which came into being and manifold were the things which came into being of Khepera. Came into being {[within Khepera]} what they {[in turn, in time] will give} gave birth to out of the creations of their offspring.

The Golden Sun Egg Uncracked
The Spiritual Meaning of Neggur
Dr Nteri Nelson

What is Khepera?
The Kemetians used this potent symbol Khepera, which powerfully expresses this Divine creative process. Khepera is pictured in the diagram at right. Khepera is a scarab beetle that lays its eggs, then rolls them up in dung and pushes them along in a ball. If we dispell* the word ball, we see that these eggs are 'ba'-lls within the greater 'Ba'-ll or Egg, that contain the germ of life, which in due course of time will become living beings. Khepera is the symbol of the One Universal Ba, or World Soul. Ba means Soul. Ba is an individualization of Spirit, which is called Ka by the Kemites (see p. 97-101 for further instruction on Ka).

Khepera is the sphericalizing (rolling form(s) into spheres) force of nature, working along with Shu and Tefnut (later described) in the creative process, i.e., a *stirring* within the formless, numberless, eggless pre-birthing sub-stance of Nu'N'.

Like that described, taking place within this symbol of Khepera terrestrially, the Kemetians intuited *Genesis* taking place Cosmically and likewise used this symbol to correspondingly express the inexpressible:

---

* For **Oracle Metaphysical Keys to Dis-Spelling Illusion see pp. 102-104.**

16 Afrikan Cosmogenesis & Cosmology of Kemet
The Nu 'N' Word

▲ sphericalizing within the Nu'N' and arising of Ra,
▲ coming into being, in the form of Khepera which,
▲ becomes, the Eye of Ra, the Cosmic Sun Egg, the One Universal Ba or Periodical Universe in total, in accord with the Law of Periodicity,
▲ simultaneous sphericalizing particularization into the many, contained *within,* the Cosmic Sun Egg, i.e.,
▲ numerous eggs which are the myriad to-be created forms, to-be birthed forth in Creation,
▲ dance of the twin forces Shu and Tefnut and the bringing forth of the All Seeing Eye of Ra and,
▲ power of Ra as Creator to Sight Itself, See Itself, As Itself, in/as All the myriad, to be birthed Life-forms, coming into manifestation, coming into Being, coming into existence.

> And likewise expressed, accordingly: ibid.
> I, even I, spat {[emitted]} Shu, [and] I emitted Tefnut, [and] I became from {[being]} one god I became three gods, that is to say, from myself two gods came into being on this earth. Were raised up therefore Shu and Tefnut in Nu (i.e., the primeval abyss of water) wherein they were. Behold, {[they, Shu and Tefnut) brought to me my eye, the Sun]} in the train of a henti period, they proceeded from me. I collected my members, they {[Shu and Tefnut]} came forth from myself after I had union with my clenched hand, came to me (?) my heart (or, will) out of my hand. The seed [which] fell into my mouth, I spat in the form of Shu, I emitted water in the form of Tefnut...

The Golden Sun Egg Uncracked
The Spiritual Meaning of Neggur
Dr Nteri Nelson

Within the waters of Nu'N', there is an arising of the Great Breath and the circumgyration within the waters of Nu'N. The fire of Ra thrills within the primordial waters of Nu'N' and the twin creative forces, called Shu & Tefnut by the Kemetians, are set to work. These are the children of Ra. They are the centripetal and centrifugal twin forces in nature producing air, heat, light (Shu) and moisture (Tefnut). Together they engage in an infolding and unfolding, play and display between themselves, like the yin and yang symbol. Through their interweaving dance, Spirit penetrates and pervades ITSELF, emanates out of ITSELF to pervade ITSELF in matter.

Just like striking a match against the flint of the box cover to light a wooden stove, the circumgyrating dance of the centripetal and centrifugal twin forces of Shu and Tefnut ignite flames within Nu'N'. The circumgyration of the fires of Ra within the waters raises a 'mound' within Nu'N'. As the fire circles, flames leap and seek to pierce the mound or 'egg,' just as the male sperm seeks to penetrate the female ovum. At last, one solitary spark leaps high above all other flames. It takes aim, makes its descent and shooting forth as a solitary Ray of the ABSOLUTE this fire penetrates and impregnates the primordial, Mother/Matter, in an explosion of effulgent Light.

18 *Afrikan Cosmogenesis & Cosmology of Kemet*
The Nu 'N' Word

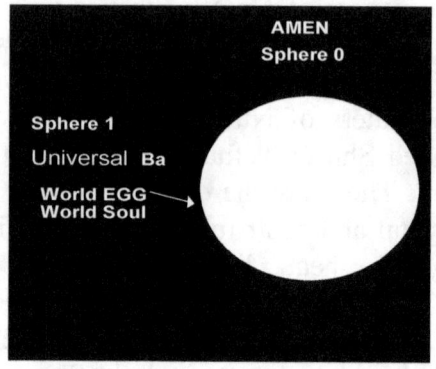

From this stirring within Nu'N', also called AMEN Sphere 0 in The Tree of Life, there is a raying forth of Light and the ONE issues forth as Creator. LIGHT is a manifestation out of DARKNESS. The coming into manifestation of Universe or Cosmos, known to our African Ancestors, would later be called *The Big Bang,* by science.

The ONE Egg, now fecundated (fertilized), is called various names by the Kemetians which include: Universal Ba, World Egg, World Soul, Cosmic Egg, Cosmic Sun, Eye of Ra. It is also called, Nginga, which is the word for seed, in the language of Kikongo, according to Dr Kimbwandende Kia Bunseki Fu-Kiau. The Cosmic Egg is humbly pictured in the diagram above, as no image can adequately capture the divine movement. This Cosmic Egg is called the Eye of Ra because it is the All Seeing and All Knowing Eye that arises out of the Nu'N' and is in the Perception, the Seeing and

The Golden Sun Egg Uncracked
The Spiritual Meaning of Neggur
Dr Nteri Nelson

Sighting of Itself, the One and the Same Self Everywhere, throughout Cosmos.

Version A

And likewise expressed, accordingly: ibid.

...Shu and Tefnut give birth to Geb and Nut. Geb and Nut give birth to Ausar, Auset, Set, Nebt-het and Heru Khent-an-maati from the womb, one after the other of them they give birth and they multiply in this earth.

Version B

...[and] behold, their children {[the children of Ausar, Auset, Set, Nebt-het and Heru Khent-an-maati]} they create beings manifold in this earth from the beings of children, from the beings of their children. They invoke my name, they overthrow their enemies, they create words of power for the overthrow of Apep, who is to be bound by the two hands of Aker, not may be his two hands, not may be his two feet, may he be chained to one place even as Ra inflicts his blows decreed for him. He is overthrown on his wicked back, slit is his face for what he hath done, and he remains upon his evil back.

▲ Cosmic Genealogy

The Neter/Netert, God/Goddess Shu and Tefnut give birth to Geb, the God of Earth pictured below at left lying underneath his wife Nut, Goddess of the sky. Shu (not shown) is the God of air between the couple. Notice the correspondence with the

20 *Afrikan Cosmogenesis & Cosmology of Kemet The Nu 'N' Word*

Masonic symbol at right, which has been taken from the Kemetic wisdom.

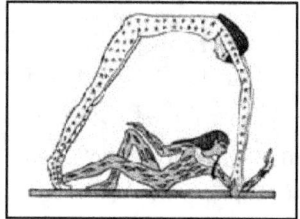

In Kemet Cosmology, Geb and Nut produced the Great Sun Egg from which the Sun-god sprang. In

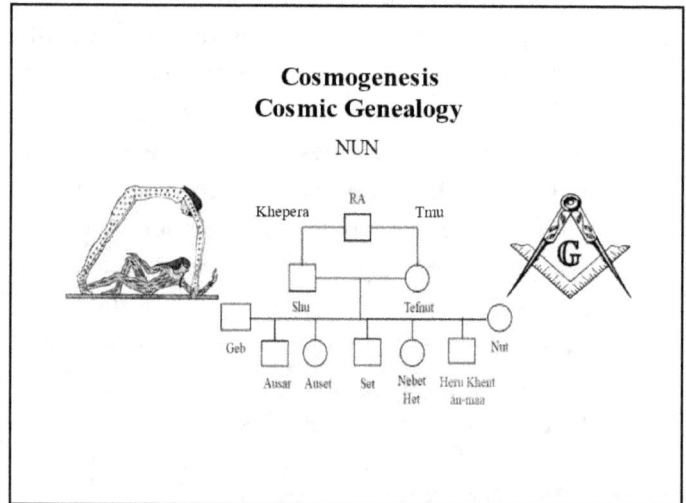

turn, Geb and Nut are Father and Mother giving birth to the Neter and Netert, (Gods and Goddesses), Ausar/Wsir, Auset, Set and Nebt-het and Heru Kent an maa (Heru The Elder).

Man and woman have all the divine attributes of God. These divine qualities or attributes are called Netcher or Netcherw, Neteru, which is the plural. Thus, man and woman are made in the Image and Likeness of/as Neter/God.

▲ **The Egg in African Cosmology and Cosmogenesis**
▲ **The Eye of Ra and The Egg Correspond**
▲ **The Goose God and The Golden Sun Egg**

In the Afrikan Cosmology of Kemet the Egg is symbolic of the entire Psycho/Spiritual Journey in Unfolding Consciousness. Here is when God the INFINITE is reflected forth as God the Creator. Thus, Universe is created with all multiplicity *within*, the all within the All. The dance of the twin forces Shu and Tefnut enables the coming into manifestation of myriad Life-forms. From this Cosmic Egg, which is the Universe, all Worlds, all creation arises. Neter/God is reflected in all that is created. Thus, Super Galaxies, Galaxies, Constellations, Suns, Planets, Moons, Man, Animals, Plants, Mineral, Atom, and down to tiniest Atomic Particle and everything in between, come into created *Being* and God transcendent becomes God indwelling.

Just as God indwells you as an individual man or woman, God indwells the Super Galaxies, Galaxies, Constellations, Suns, Planets, Moons, Man, Animals, Plants, Mineral, Atoms, and so on, down to tiniest Atomic Particle, everything in between, and up to and including the Universe in total, called the Universal Ba.

Therefore, Ba is tiniest Atom and sub Atomic Particles, Ba is ultimately Universe and Ba is everything in between. So we can see that, there is Ba within Ba within Ba, Egg within Egg within Egg, Eye within Eye within Eye, Sun within Sun within Sun, Seed within Seed within Seed. This is expressed in the Great Scale of Being diagram that follows:

The Golden Sun Egg Uncracked
The Spiritual Meaning of Neggur

Dr Nteri Nelson

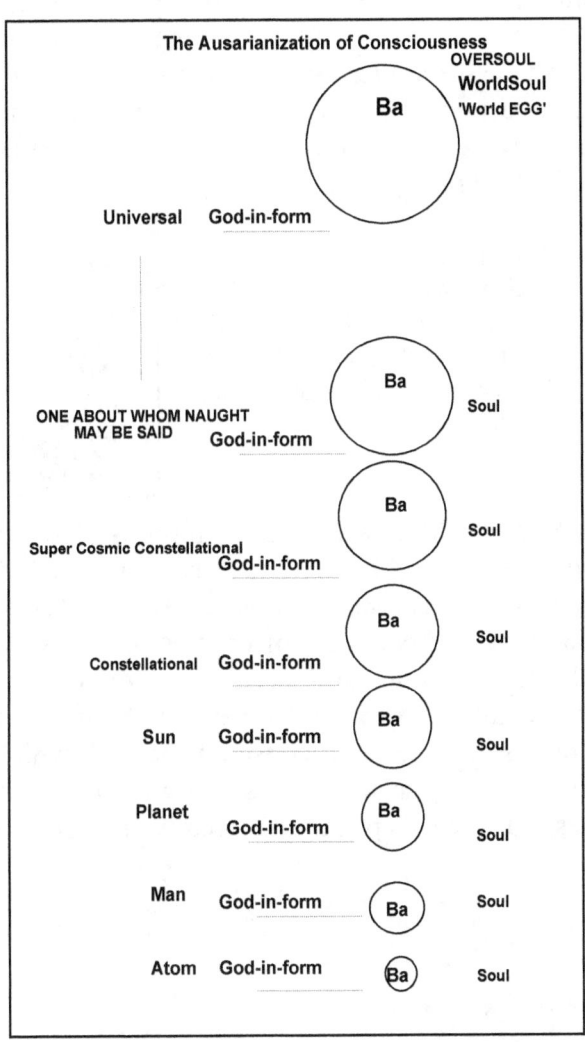

Let's appreciate the limitation in any diagram representing the evolutionary advancement in consciousness. In these representations, innumerable entities on every rung of the evolutionary ladder of conscious Spiritual development are left out (as no name is known). Nevertheless, the idea is to see the same *'essential'* Ba at every level of its immersion in form/Matter. This is expressed accordingly: E.A. Wallis Budge. *The Gods of the Egyptians, V.II,* p. 299.

> The mythological and religious texts contain indications that the Egyptians believed in what may be described as a "World-Soul," which they called Ba; its symbol was a bearded man-headed hawk...

This Kemetic Medew Netcher symbol is pictured in the diagram at right: The Universal Ba is inclusive of each successive Ba. Each successive Ba takes its place along a great scale of entities, both vast and small. Each Ba is an individualization of Spirit. Spirit is called Ka by the Kemetians. As such, each Ba, represents a level of conscious activity which is called Soul by the Kemetians. Ka and Nu'N' have correspondence as primordial creative sub-stance.

The Golden Sun Egg Uncracked 25
The Spiritual Meaning of Neggur
Dr Nteri Nelson

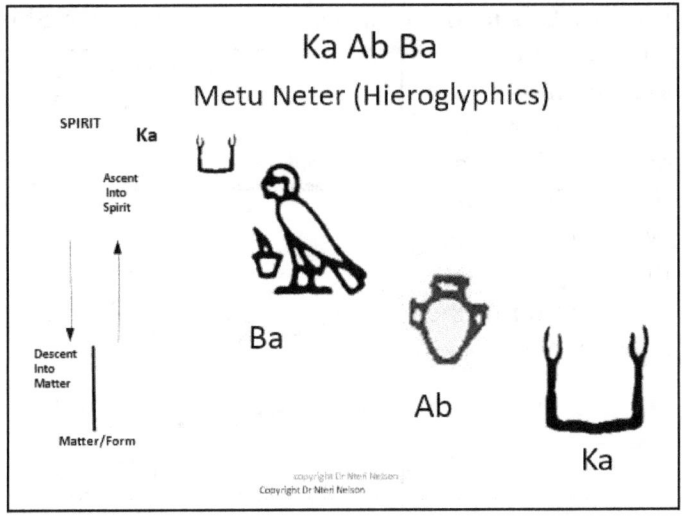

There is that which is **KaAbBa** within *each* **Ba**, at every level of its immersion in Matter/form, at every level of and along the grand scale of Creation. For further instruction see pp. 95-101 and the entire book on this subject matter entitled: KaAbBa Building The Lighted Temple Metaphysical Keys To The Tree Of Life by Dr Nteri Nelson.

▲ Our Planetary Earth God Geb

On the Planetary scale of existence or more 'local' level of Cosmos, the dance of the twin forces Shu and Tefnut enables the coming into manifestation of our Planetary Earth God, Geb. We locate the Planetary Earth God Geb on in the diagram above:

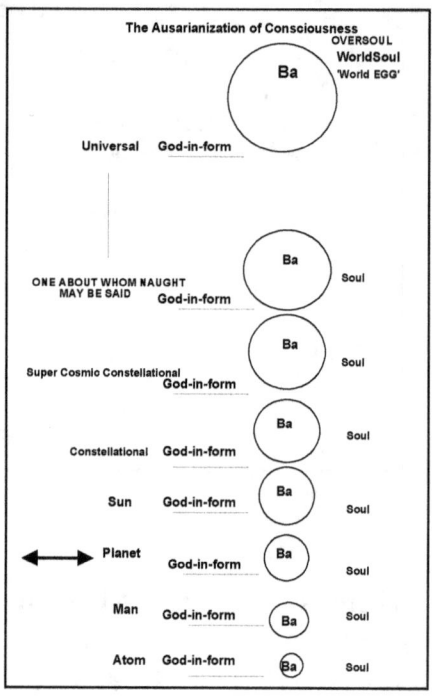

The Planetary Egg of Earth Humanity
The Birth of Individual and Collective Consciousness

The Golden Goose on the head of Geb is a symbol of fertility, virility and generativity. The goose eggs, symbolize the birth of humanity, or more accurately, the individual and collective consciousness of humanity. It is in the orb and watch of Geb that

The Golden Sun Egg Uncracked
The Spiritual Meaning of Neggur
Dr Nteri Nelson

we come before the scales of Maat in the Hall of Judgment that our Soul may be weighed. Accordingly: E.A. Wallis Budge. *The Gods of the Egyptians, V.II,* p. 95-96.

> He is one of the company of the gods who watch the weighing of the heart of the deceased in the Judgment Hall of Ausar, and on his brow rested the secret gates which were close by the Balance of Ra, and which were guarded by the god himself. The righteous who were provided the necessary words of power were enabled to make their escape from the earth wherein their bodies were laid, but the wicked were held fast by Geb.

▲ **The Names of Geb and The Goose Who Laid The Golden Sun Egg are Variously Translated as** **'Negg-ur' 'Negneg ur', 'Gengen ur'** and seen in the following Medew Netcher language which would later be called Hieroglyphics by the Greeks:

The Nu 'N' Word

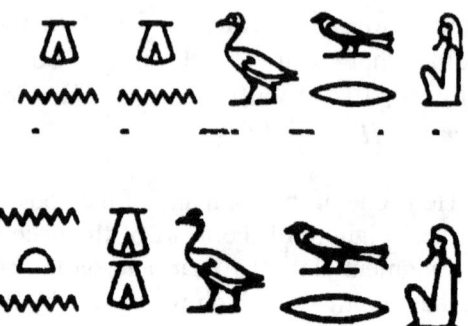

▲ Medew Netcher Language

The Kemetians (later called Egyptians by the Greeks) used picture images or ideographs from nature all around them to communicate ideas. This language is called Mdw Ntr or Medew Netcher - a name which means, 'divine words and speech of the Gods'. This word is variously spelled and some of the forms are as follows: Mtu Ntr, Mdw Ntr, Metu Neter, Medew Netjer, Medew Netger and so on. The Ancient Wisdom of our Afrikan Ancestors tells us that letters are sacred and Divine Beings. Letters are Oracles of God, acting as divine messages and messengers.

These are the Ntr, Netcher, Netcherw and known as qualities of Divinity, also many call, God. Words are constructed by putting letters or Netcherw together, that make up a 'name', sound a vibration and convey quality(ies) of divinity. The primal consonants are used to make up a word and convey its meaning and various vowels are added, substituted, and/or subtracted before or after

The Golden Sun Egg Uncracked
The Spiritual Meaning of Neggur
Dr Nteri Nelson

consonants which lend themselves to facility in pronunciation.

▲ **How is this name transliterated (translated)?**

With and without vowels added, this name is sounded: **NGGR, NGNGUR, GNGNUR** or **NEGGUR, NEGNEGUR, GENGENUR** and is spelled using the Medew Netcher alphabet and ideagraph symbols as follows:

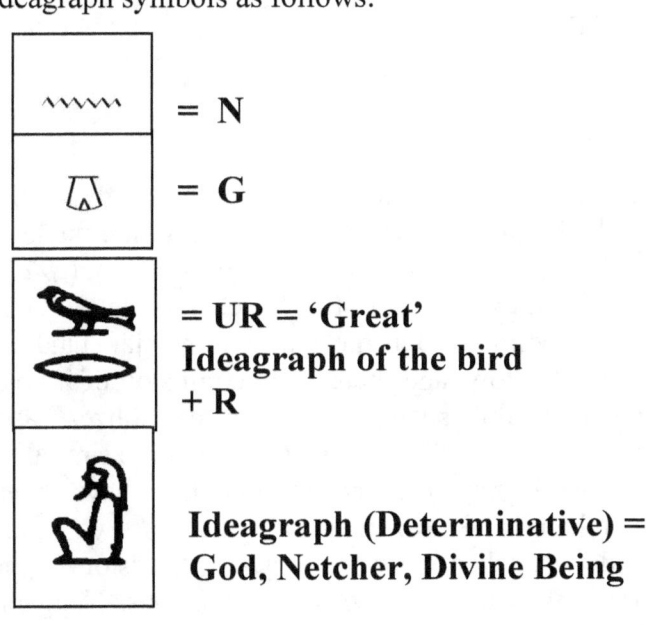

▲ **Kenken ur, Neknek ur**

E.A. Wallace Budge translates this name variously, as you have just seen the names, Negg ur, Negneg ur and Gengen ur from his Hieroglyphic Dictionary. In the following pages you will see inscriptions written in the Medew Netcher language followed by Budge's translations. In these instances you will see this name translated as, 'Kenken ur' or 'Neknek ur'. This use of the Netcher or letter 'K' is not shown in the name when we refer to the actual Medew Netcher inscriptions from which the text is interpreted from; and whose alphabet symbol for K, Q, or C would be as follows:

◿	= K, Q
⌣	= K, C

The instances of Budge spelling the name of the Earth God as, Kenken ur or Neknek ur, are unclear. In the, *Egyptian Grammar Study of Hieroglyphics* by Sir Alan Gardiner, the Netcher or letter G is clearly symbolized as the symbol for a 'jar stand' as pictured below, and there is no confusion of it with any other alphabet symbol. Also symbolizes base, throne, or stool. That, G, K, C and Q give similarity of sound may be one reason they have been interchanged. Since, it is not spelled as such in the Medew Netcher text written by our Ancestors in the inscriptions that follow, only the names, Negg ur, Negneg ur, Gengen ur, will be used in this book, beyond the aforementioned instances.

The Golden Sun Egg Uncracked
The Spiritual Meaning of Neggur
Dr Nteri Nelson

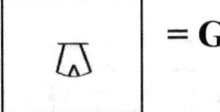 = G

▲ Medew Netcher Verses
In the verses that follow from the, *Prt Em Hru. The Book of Coming Forth By Day,* which would later be titled, *The Egyptian Book of The Dead*, we read the name and story of Geb, the Goose God: p. 446, 447.

Afrikan Cosmogenesis & Cosmology of Kemet
The Nu 'N' Word

> **CHAPTER LIV**
> THE CHAPTER OF GIVING AIR
> **PLATE XV**
>
> [hieroglyphic text]

1. THE CHAPTER OF GIVING AIR IN KHERT-NETER. The Osiris Ani saith:—I am the Egg which dwelt in the Great Cackler. I keep ward over that great 2. place which Keb hath proclaimed upon earth. I live; it liveth. I grow up, I live, I snuff the air. I am 3. Utchā-aāb. I go round about his egg [to protect it]. I have thwarted the moment of Set. 4. Hail, Sweet one of the Two Lands! Hail, dweller in the *tchefa* food! Hail, dweller in the lapis lazuli (*i.e.*, the blue sky?)! Watch ye over him that is in his cradle (literally nest), the Babe when he cometh forth to you.

The Golden Sun Egg Uncracked
The Spiritual Meaning of Neggur
Dr Nteri Nelson

An Older Version of this Chapter is found in the Papyrus of Nu (Sheet 12), the text of which reads: -

CHAPTER LIV. 1. THE CHAPTER OF GIVING AIR 2. TO NU IN KHERT-NETER. He saith :—Hail, thou God Temu, grant thou unto me the sweet breath which dwelleth in thy nostrils! I am the Egg 3. which is in Kenken-ur (*i.e.*, the Great Cackler), and I watch and guard that mighty thing which hath come into being, wherewith the god Keb hath opened the earth. I live; it liveth; 4. I grow, I live, I snuff the air. I am the god Utchā-aābet, and I go about his egg. I shine at the moment of 5. the mighty of strength, Suti. Hail, thou who makest sweet the time (?) of the two Lands! Hail, dweller among the celestial food.

Hail, dweller among the beings of blue (or, lapis lazuli), watch ye to protect him that is in 6. his nest (*i.e.*, cradle), the Child who cometh forth to you.

CHAPTER LIX

CHAPTER OF SNUFFING THE AIR IN KHERT-NETER

PLATE XVI

[hieroglyphic text]

1. THE CHAPTER OF SNUFFING THE AIR, AND OF HAVING POWER OVER THE WATER IN KHERT-NETER. The Osiris Ani saith:—Hail, thou Sycamore tree of the goddess Nut! Give me of the [water and of the] air 2. which is in thee. I embrace that throne which is in Unu,[1] and I keep guard over 3. the Egg of Neḳeḳ-ur.[2] It flourisheth, and I flourish[3]; it liveth and I live; 4. it snuffeth the air, and I snuff the air, I the Osiris Ani, whose word is truth, in [peace].

[1] The town of Hermopolis, the chief god of which was, as its name signifies, Thoth.

[2] Other forms of the name are [hieroglyphs] and [hieroglyphs]. This god is Ḳeb, the Earth-god. The Egg is the sun.

[3] The meaning is, "if the Egg flourisheth, then I shall flourish; if it liveth, I shall live; if it snuffeth the air, I shall snuff the air; if it doth not flourish, nor live, nor snuff the air, then I shall do none of these things and shall die.

CHAPTER LVI. 1. [hieroglyphic text] 2. [hieroglyphic text] 3. [hieroglyphic text]

The Golden Sun Egg Uncracked
The Spiritual Meaning of Neggur
Dr Nteri Nelson

> CHAPTER LVI. THE CHAPTER OF SNUFFING THE AIR 2. WITH WATER IN KHERT-NETER. Hail, Tem. Grant thou unto me the sweet breath which dwelleth in thy nostrils. I am he who embraceth that great throne 3. which is in the city of Unu (*i.e.*, Hermopolis). I keep watch over the

> Egg of Kenken-ur (*i.e.*, the Great Cackler). I grow and flourish [as] it groweth and flourisheth. 4. I live [as] it liveth. I snuff the air [as] it snuffeth the air (or, my breath is its breath).

In these verses we can see the intimacy involved in the care of the Egg and how it may be diminished or enhanced by the degree of its safeguarding. Unlike the 'material' nest egg we may try to protect in guarding our wealth, money or physical well being on Earth, Geb is how we are guarding our 'Spiritual' wealth in developing our nest egg of wisdom, or the all seeing eye. It is the Sun in each of us. This is initiation.

▲ Developing Planetary Consciousness
What is Initiation?

Initiation is the successive process of expansion in consciousness, which is our return to the inner-sightedness of the whole. It is the opening of our 1st eye. It is your growing awareness upon 'each' of the 7 planes of consciousness (latter described) as you make your 'conscious re-ascent.' Initiation by initiation you ascend the 'rungs of the ladder' up the Tree of Life. With each 'rung' upward you are sounding a Higher Spiritual vibration, a higher appeal. Each sounding is the release of the encapsulated 'lesser self' on the way to embracing more - the One True Self. It is through these stages of initiation that so-called secrets are again revealed whereby man 're-members' how to put his 'broken consciousness' back together again - thus realizing, the Unity of Spirit. Today the initiate must move through stages of initiation in his re-ascent up the Tree of Life where full Sun-Son/Daughter is revealed. Wsir/Ausarian resurrection is a return to Unity or God consciousness. A consciousness we left when we 'seemingly' left our Father's Home.

• In the ages that would lead man and woman in their Involutionary descent and despiritualization in consciousness.

• The 'ways' of innate inner knowingness and wholeness would become the veiled and concealed 'secrets' withheld from the masses of humanity, leaving them to *grope* in the dark, blinded, trying to find 'their way Home.

Man and woman are confined to the womb and the tomb upon the Wheel of Birth and Death until they undergo Earth's initiations. When these Initiations are attained one is able to get off of the wheel and thus freely come and go between the Heavenly and Earthly realms.

As one human family we make up the collective consciousness of our Earth that has been evolving over eons of time. On a higher turn of the spiral, the collective consciousness in the human family may be expressing itself at its Spiritually, optimal and divine level. On a lower turn of the spiral, the collective consciousness in the human family may be expressing itself at its most, materially debased and despiritualized level. Our personal and collective will, thought, desire, choice and action is either working in or out of accord with the Divine Will, Love, Intelligence and Law that is guiding our Earth into a greater measure of light. Our choices determine how *and if* we are manifesting the Kingdom of God on Earth. We are the evolving Planetary Mind as symbolized by the Sun God Egg in the diagram at right:

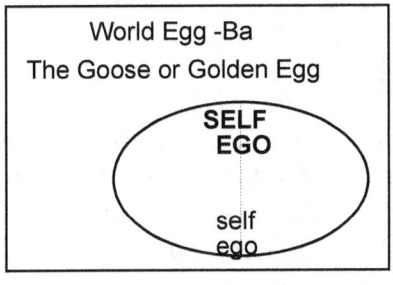

No matter what Root Race one 'belongs to' this collective consciousness, which now pervades our Planetary consciousness, is the province in which all humanity must work to re-Spiritualize, clear and cleanse of its accumulated darkness. Presently as Earth inhabitants, we are attaining *to-be* conscious as the God indwelling the Planet is conscious. Through your expanding consciousness as man or woman, your attainment to Planetary consciousness enables you to 'come forth' and say, 'I and my Father are One' – *'Nuk Wsir/Ausar'* which is Kemetic for, *'I am Wisir/Ausar'*. *Wsir/Ausar*

symbolizes the Lord of the World whom all humanity must come before to be found 'True of voice'.

▲ **Negg, Negaga** - **To cackle to quack.**
In continuing to dispel the names of the Sun God Egg, Negg ur, Negneg ur, Gengen ur, we see accordingly: E.A. Wallis Budge. *An Egyptian Hieroglyphic Dictionary,* p. 398
Negg, Negaga - To cackle to quack.
Nega – cackler.
Meaning:
Called the Great Cackler, the goose is the great 'clocker'. The goose cackles and this arousing sound starts time and keeps time. This is similar to the rooster who cackles and arouses one from sleep. The Golden Sun Egg represents a time-space continuum on our Planetary Earth Plane. The culmination of the Egg is to sound the fullness of the Vibration of the One True Self, as the God ensouling the Earth – Geb. Understanding the Sun God Egg, Negg ur, Negneg ur, Gengen ur, brings us to the basic game in unfolding consciousness and Wsir/Ausarian Resurrection. It is a game you know well called 'Hide and Go Seek.'

▲ **Let's Review How The Game of** *Hide and Go Seek* **Played**
Players: In the Game of Hide and Go Seek you are the One True Self who 'seemingly' projects a 'self'- which is the same One Self - that then goes and hides. As you go hide the same, one self, under a

The Golden Sun Egg Uncracked
The Spiritual Meaning of Neggur
Dr Nteri Nelson

bush and *forget* the, One True Self, that you are - your Soul Light becomes dimmed.

Object of the Game:
1. The *self* goes out to hide while the *Self* remains at Base and counts or *cackles*, thus keeping time.
2. The Cackler is the clocker. The self moves out in a ring-pass-not of activity or circle defined by space and time. The clocker counts off, 1, 2, 3, 4, 5 and so on, up to some finite number. When that number is reached the Self goes out to find the self.
3. Meanwhile the self is also looking to find the Self, and make its return back Home to Base. If the Self spots the self and reaches Base *first,* it shouts, 'I got your goose'. If the self can get back to Home Base first, it then shouts, 'I got my goose'.
4. What have we 'got' in playing this game? We are re-uniting the EGO with the ego, which falsely came to believe itself as separate. We get our Egg, our Ego, back together again.
5. The Sun within a Greater Sun, the Egg within a Greater Egg.

In referring to the diagram at right:

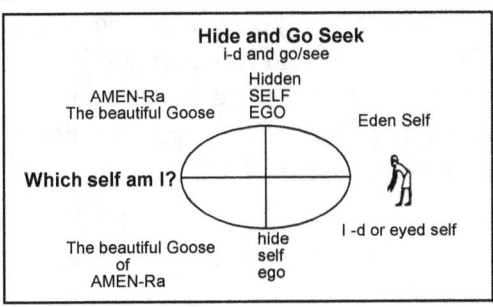

1. Above the horizontal line or horizon we see the Self be-fore it *goes out to see Itself* reflected in the' seeming other self. The interiorly focused SELF - remains resident in the Spiritual world, *while* operating in the Physical World through the use of mental, emotional and physical Soul bodies.
2. Below the horizontal line we see the 'self' - that 'seemingly' has gone out'. The exteriorly focused self – can 'forget' it residence in the Spiritual realm. This self is now hiding under bush or skin of material form. Such hiding blots out or obscures the Light of the Soul, called Ba, or the Sun within.

▲ What is The Metaphysical Meaning of The Game Hide and Go Seek?

•The *Self* is Eternal - that which we are and have always been from the beginningless beginning.
•The *self* is what we have hidden under coats of skin or a bush.
•These coats of skin are the physical, emotional and mental Soul bodies.
•We hide under flesh in the physical body, and think we are it.
•We hide under glamour of emotions such as: fear, desire, loss, anger, greed, etc. and think we are it.
•We hide under our thoughtforms, all the thinking about thing-ness in our minds, and thinking the self into less and less, and think we are it.
•Where is the true Self to be found under all of this game playing that deludes and diminishes us into a lesser sense of Self?

The Golden Sun Egg Uncracked
The Spiritual Meaning of Neggur
Dr Nteri Nelson

- It is a game that has us thinking the Self as separated and isolated, from the One True Self.
- How could this be when IT *is* the same One True Self which is in all Selves?
- The self that is seeking, and the Self that is sought, *are One*.
- Like the Prodigal Son/Daughter, you just had to *go-see or goose* for yourself.
- We go hide then we must seek the self that we have hidden.
- As the One Self urges the other 'seeming self(s)' to return, the hiding self is stimulated to return and touch goose - Aha!

▲ What is the Divine Trinity, Wsir/Ausar, Auset, Heru?

The story of the Divine Trinity pre-dates Christianity by thousands of years. For a fuller version of the story refer to, *Ka Ab Ba Building The Lighted Temple*. Briefly, for our purposes here, it is important to understand that as the eldest race, *Our story* is an ancient story. Furthermore, within Our story, other stories have been enfolded, encoded and evolved over time. Thus Our Story is *story, within story, within story*. The story of Wsir/Ausar, Auset and Heru is one such story. Wsir/Ausar, Auset and Heru are later called Osiris, Isis, and Horus, respectively by the Greeks. The Greeks and others re-named much of our story. For our purposes now the question is:

▲ How Does The Story of Wsir/Ausar, Auset and Heru Contribute in Telling About The Egg of Human and Collective Consciousness in Man and Woman?

We are told by the Ancient Wisdom in the story of Wsir/Ausar, Auset and Heru, that:
1. Wsir/Ausar and Auset harmoniously rule their kingdom as King and Queen.
2. Heru is the son of Wsir/Ausar and Auset.
3. Wsir/Ausar is slain by his jealous brother Set, his body cut and broken into fourteen pieces.
4. A fierce battle ensues between Heru and Set in which Heru must avenge his Father's death and be restored as the rightful heir to the throne. This symbolizes the re-establishing of the Kingdom of God on Earth.

▲ When the Golden Sun Egg is Uncracked

Heru is that aspect of your Spiritual Faculty where you are linking the Spiritual nature with the Physical/Material nature - both within you. Heru is the second aspect of the Divine Trinity of Wsir/Ausar Heru and Auset, which dwells within you. We will see that this relating by the Heru aspect in you is how you find your way back Home after you have made your descent down the Tree of Life. This is expressed accordingly by: Gerald Massey. *Ancient Egypt. The Light of The World*, p. 892.

> In his birth he says, "I am the babe" born as the connecting link betwixt earth and heaven, and as the one who does not die the second death (ch.42). **He issues from the disc or from the egg. He is**

The Golden Sun Egg Uncracked
The Spiritual Meaning of Neggur
Dr Nteri Nelson

pursued by the Herrut-reptile, but, as he says, his egg remains unpierced by the destroyer.

For the Egg to remain unpierced, is to remain uncracked and unbroken, This is derived from the Ritual Text of the *Prt Em Hru* which is further expressed accordingly: E.A. Wallis Budge. *The Egyptian Book of The Dead*, p. 356.

> I come forth and advance and my name is unknown. I am yesterday, and my name is 'Seer of millions of years.' I travel, I travel along the path of Heru the Judge. I am the lord of eternity; I feel and I have power to perceive. I am the lord of the red crown. I am the Sun's eye, yea, **I am in my egg, in my egg.** It is granted unto me to live therewith. **I am in the Sun's eye**, when it closeth, and I live by the strength thereof. I come forth and I shine; I enter in and I come to life. **I am in the Sun's eye, my seat is on my throne, and I sit thereon with the eye.** I am Heru who pass through millions of years. I have governed my throne and I rule it by the words of my mouth; and whether [I] speak or whether [I] keep silence, I keep the balance even. Verily my forms are changed. I am the god Unen, from season unto season; what is mine is with me. **I am the only One born of an only One.**

As Heru we may all affirm: *I am the only One born of an only One.* This is Biblically expressed as the 'Only begotten Son'. We find reference to, Negg ur, Negneg ur, Gengen ur, in the, *The Kingdom of Khenti-Amenti Ausar The Second Division Of The*

Tuat. It is clear from the following that those referenced are diminished in their state of 'Eggness', and have fallen out of favor. They are bowed, bound and broken. This is expressed accordingly: E.A. Wallis Budge. *The Egyptian Heaven & Hell*, p. 119:

> Turning now to those beings who stand to the left of the Boat (vol. ii., pp. 96-99), we see that they are twenty-four in number; of these four lie dead, or helpless, and are called ENENIU, i.e., the "Inert," and twenty stand with their backs bowed, and their arms tied at their elbows behind them, in an agonizing position. Here, it is clear, are beings who are fettered and stand awaiting their doom. The charges made against them are to the effect that: 1. They blasphemed Ra upon earth. 2. They invoked evil upon him that was in the Egg. 3. They thrust aside the right. 4. They spoke against KHUTI.
>
> The god referred to as being "in the Egg" is, of course, a form of the Sun-god, and we know from the LIVth Chapter of the Book of the Dead, that the EGG was laid by KENKENUR, or the "Great Cackler." The good KHUTI is the form of the Sun-god at sunrise and sunset, and thus we see that all the sins which were committed by the ENENIU and their fettered companions were against Ra, and against forms of him. The name given to these is "STAU," i.e., "Apostates of the Hall of Ra," and sentence of doom is passed upon them by TEMU on behalf of Ra; it is decreed that their arms shall never be untied again, that their bodies shall be cut to pieces, and that their souls shall cease to exist (vol. ii., p. 97). Such are the things which take

The Golden Sun Egg Uncracked
The Spiritual Meaning of Neggur
Dr Nteri Nelson

place in the Second Division of the Tuat according to the BOOK OF GATES, and, view them in whatever way we may, it is impossible not to conclude that the Egyptians thought that those who praised and worshipped Ra upon earth were rewarded with good things, whilst those who treated him lightly were punished. It is evident also that the offering up of propitiatory sacrifices and making of peace offerings were encouraged by the religion of Osiris, as being good both for gods and men.

▲ How Did The Sun Egg Become Cracked Remember the Childhood Jingle Humpty Dumpty?

The following nursery rhyme reflects the brokenness, separation and part-i-cularization in consciousness operative within man and woman and between the human family on our Planet today. It is 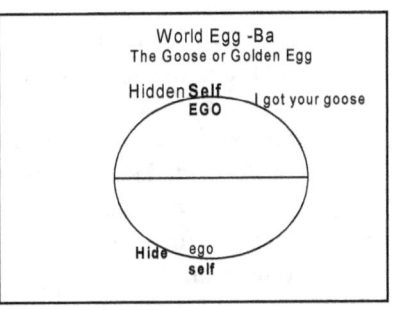 the result of the descent down the Tree of Life and becoming forgetful of our Image and Likeness of God - The One True Self.

"Humpty Dumpty
Sat on a wall
Humpty Dumpty
Had a Great Fall

All the King's horses and all the King's men
Couldn't put Humpty together again"

▲ Negengen
In continuing to dispel the names of the Sun God Egg, Negg ur, Negneg ur, Gengen ur, we see accordingly: E.A. Wallis Budge. *An Egyptian Hieroglyphic Dictionary,* Vol. 1 p. 398.
Negengen – To destroy or break in pieces. (We will further dispel this word shortly).
Meaning:
Negengen becomes a state of brokenness of the Sun God Egg Negg ur, Negneg ur, Gengen ur. This change in the state of wholeness in consciousness is expressed accordingly: Alvin Boyd Kuhn. *The Lost Light,* p. 375, in a prayer that Wsir/Ausar may,

> 'be saved from the attack made against him "at the crossing." (ch.135). This indicates that assault on his young divinity is made as soon as he crosses the line on the west in his descent. He is then **"the youngling in the egg"** and subject to the Herut attack. Here the dragon lays in wait to devour the young child'.

And likewise, expressed accordingly: E. A. Wallis Budge. *The Prt Em Hru. (Egyptian Book Of The Dead),* Chap. XXXlV, p. 340.

> My nest is not seen, **and I have not broken [read here: cracked] my egg.** I am lord of millions of years. I have made my nest in the uttermost parts of heaven. I have come

down unto the earth of Seb [read here: Geb, Keb]

▲ The Cracked God Egg

The Cracked God Egg symbolizes fragmented or broken God Consciousness It is the eye that sees in part and not in wholeness. What is the battle involved in defending the Egg from being diminished, attacked, broken?

1. Like the cracked Egg, the brokenness of the body of Wsir/Ausar is a key, symbolizing the brokenness in man and woman's consciousness of the Divinity within.
2. It is likewise a symbol of the brokenness, separation and part-I-cularization in consciousness of the Divinity within the human family.
3. It is the result of the descent down the Tree of Life and the converging cycle(s) of time, which make up *The Perfect Storm,* latter described, in which we now live.

Does this give insight into why Whites find it so insulting to be so called 'Crackers' by so called 'Negroes'? Are Whites seen, on some deep psycho-spiritual level, as having 'cracked the Egg'? To understand this seeming 'descent' in consciousness, we must understand the Law of Vibration.

▲ What is the Law of Vibration?

The Ancients knew that:

48 Afrikan Cosmogenesis & Cosmology of Kemet The Nu 'N' Word

1. All is Spirit and that Spirit periodically seeks to know ITSELF by reflecting itself into its dual aspect of Spirit-Matter.
2. Spirit is matter at its lowest level of vibration and Matter is Spirit at its highest level of vibration. (See *The Kybalion; Secret Doctrine*)
3. All in Universe is vibration.
4. Spirit vibrates at the highest, fastest most refined level.
5. Matter vibrates at a lower, slower more coarse or dense level.

This is indicated in the diagram at right:

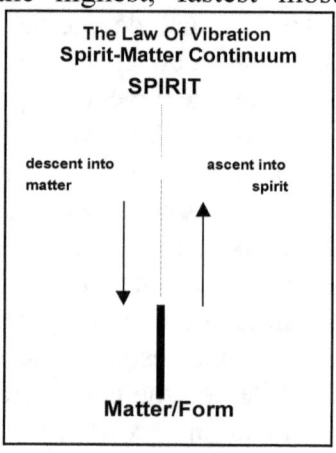

▲ Involutionary and Evolutionary Cycles

The Law of Vibration is seen operative along the Spirit-Matter continuum in what is called the involutionary and evolutionary cycles of human consciousness. The involutionary and evolutionary cycles are pictured in the diagram at right:

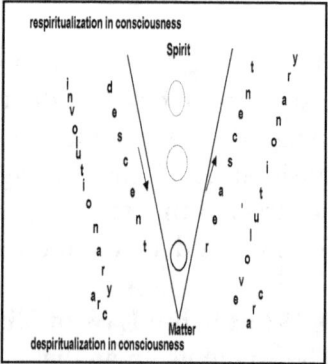

On the involutionary arc, consciousness makes its descent from the Spiritual, becoming more materialized. The vertex

The Golden Sun Egg Uncracked
The Spiritual Meaning of Neggur
Dr Nteri Nelson

in the 'V' illustrates how Spirit has made its deepest descent into matter. On the evolutionary arc, consciousness is making its return ascent and becomes re-spiritualized. Taken together, this is the involutionary and evolutionary cycle of human consciousness.

▲ **What is This Line You Cross in Consciousness? Crossing the Line and Death**

In the diagram at right we see the Golden Sun Egg or Ba. We also see the equinoctial line that has been drawn and denotes:

a. Division of the circle/egg in half, demarking East and West.
b. The horizon - which marks the Sun's passage by day and by night.

When you go out to 'hide' in your involutionary descent in consciousness you cross over the equinoctial line. Thus you enter the more dense material realm. This is indicated by the dotted line in the diagram:

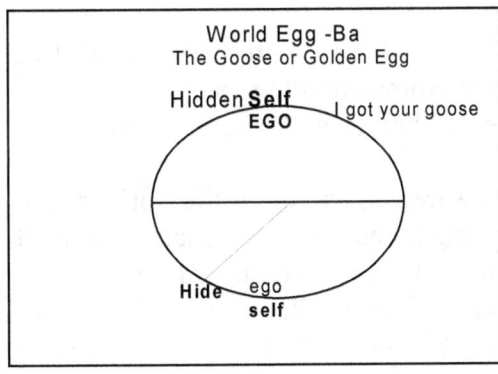

▲ Crossing over into Form/Manifestation
The precipitation into Form

Moving from left to right in the diagrams below, we see consciousness before it has crossed over the horizon to now make its descent along the Spirit-matter continuum into the more material

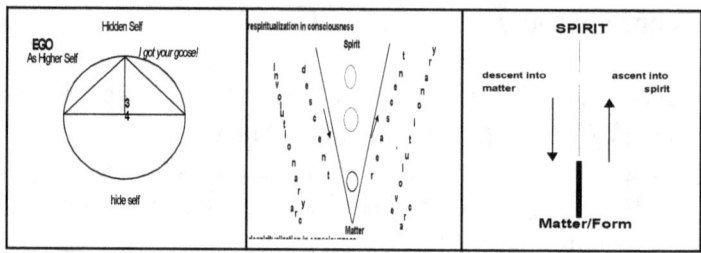

consciousness.

What is this line 'On the West" You Cross in Consciousness?

- The line is the 4th plane of consciousness in your Spiritual equipment
- It is the horizon where the Sun both rises and sets
- It is the balance point on the scales of justice Maat - sphere 4, in the Tree of Life
- It is the equinox where dark and light are held in balance.
- It is this line where we are 'seemingly' divided and made both Human and Divine.
- It is the diaphragm in the human body.

If your awareness is below the horizon it is below the diaphragm and under the coats of skin which are called the physical, emotional, and mental Soul bodies. The Chakras below the diaphragm are the Base, the Sacral, and the Solar Plexus. It is the crossing over of Spirit into the material realm. If

The Golden Sun Egg Uncracked
The Spiritual Meaning of Neggur
Dr Nteri Nelson

you forget your citizenship in the Higher realms, you become the particulate self, encapsulated under coats of skin. This is expressed accordingly: H. P. Blavatsky. *The Veil of Isis* [read here: - The Veil of Auset], V. 1, p. 2.

> As the cycle proceeded, man's eyes were more and more opened, until he came to know "good and evil" as well as the Elohim themselves. Having reached its summit, the cycle began to go downward. When the arc attained a certain point which brought it parallel with the fixed line of our terrestrial plane, the man was furnished by nature with "coats of skin," and the Lord God "clothed them.

The Following Analogy Will Serve to Aid Our Understanding of the Above Quote:

If we put a tablespoon of sugar into a glass of water and stir it, the sugar dissolves and cannot be seen or detected in the water with the naked eye. If we repeat the process we have the same finding. However, if we continue the process of adding, then stirring in tablespoon after tablespoon of sugar to the water, we will reach a point of saturation and some measure of the particles of sugar will no longer stay in the solution. Anyone who has made lemonade or likes their coffee sweet knows this Metaphysical principle which is revealed in the diagram at right and aptly expressed in the following accordingly:

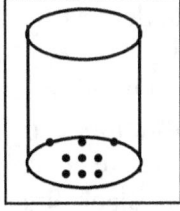

- Today in consciousness as a humanity we sit as one particulate after another
- In our limited, gran-ulated, encapsulated view of our-selves at the bottom of the glass
- We identify as the limited 'I' or ego that has to get 'somewhere' as one 'seeming" separate self, encounters another 'seeming', separate self
- The lower fire - *fire by friction* - is at work in road rage with other particulates or separate selves along the way, as we fend for this limited sense of 'self'
- In rotary motion at the bottom of the glass, we spin our wheels violating the Laws of Right Relationship - Maat
- To access the higher fire of Ra - *Solar Fire and Electric fire* we must enter into Meditation - also called Trance
- The process of Meditation is like taking the spoon and stirring all the particularizations, which is 'ourselves' - *back into solution*
- This stirring is our access to the cohering power of Tehuti and fuller vibrational sounding of Seker
- When all particularization is held seamlessly in solution and we *hold* within our 1st Eye we are at once able to witness the whole moving geometry in the Mind of God and know the *solution* to all life's challenges

If vibration can cause things to fall apart then vibration can likewise cause that which has been separate to cohere and come back together. When the Black Race comes back to the Ancient wisdom teachings, then we will be counted among the ranks

The Golden Sun Egg Uncracked
The Spiritual Meaning of Neggur
Dr Nteri Nelson

of those sounding the harmonious sound that unites not only Black people but all people and therefore re-elevates the consciousness of the Human family into the Spiritual Kingdom.

▲ Neg

In continuing to dispel the names of the Sun God Egg, Negg-ur, Negneg ur, GenGen ur, we see accordingly: E.A. Wallis Budge. *An Egyptian Hieroglyphic Dictionary,* p. 398

Neg – A bull, the four horned bull, god of heaven, to cackle.

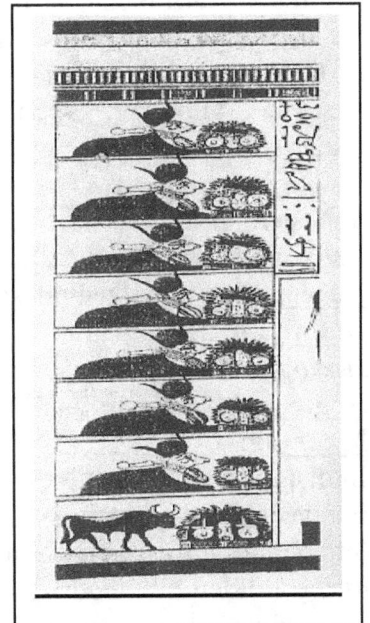

Meaning: Like the Egg, the Bull and the Cow are symbols of generativity, virility and fertility.

The Ancients were very familiar with the 7 planes or Arits of consciousness. Pictured in the diagram on the next page, from the Papyrus of Ani, are the 7 Het-Heru or celestial cow goddesses. Het-Heru is also known as Hathor. Like the floors in an elevator ride, each represents a plane in consciousness, a vib-rational field, that must be ascended by the Neg, or Bull of Heaven, who is pictured at the bottom, and is you and me. Het-Heru glimpses the inner archetypal patterning of greater wholeness and beauty *upon each plane and* causes us - the Initiate - to aspire towards the divinely intended design. It is important to remember that even though we are looking at 7 'seemingly' discrete divisions in con-sciousness, the only separation is the one created by our own illusion of separative or broken consciousness. When we are using the Het-Heru/Hathor part of our Spiritual equip-ment at a higher turn of the spiral or optimal level, we are magnetically attracting the higher ideal to be manifested in our lives. We are then wise and unbroken when we maintain the integrity of the Neg or Egg or Ego.

▲ **Negengen**
Let's now revisit and further dispel the word Negengen as previously described.
Definition: E.A. Wallis Budge. *An Egyptian Hieroglyphic Dictionary*, p. 398.
Negengen - to destroy or break in pieces.
Meaning:
In dispelling the word Ne-gen gen we see that it reveals 'reduplication' of the Netcherw or letters and similarity in 'sound' to the names of the Golden Sun God – Negg ur, Negneg ur, Gengen ur.

▲ **Negg ur**
Let's continue to dispel the word Neggur:

The Golden Sun Egg Uncracked
The Spiritual Meaning of Neggur
Dr Nteri Nelson

What does the word sound like? Say the word out loud and then silently in a meditative state.

Derived Sounds Like List:
Neggur -The goose-goddess who laid the sun-egg, the bull, the four, horned bull, god of heaven, the cackler sounds like Negre, Niger or Nigger

Meaning:
Is it possible that the word Negro, Niger or Nigger may have older origin in its meaning than the 'negative' 16th century one so familiar to the so called 'modern World'? If so, it is important to point our youth to this ancient harmonic.

▲ Could There Be a Harmonic Relationship Between the Word Negg ur, Negneg ur, Gengen ur and The Words Negro, Nigger?

On July 9, 2007 the NAACP took steps to - 'bury the 'N' word' - in a ritualistic and ceremonial way. This was a significant step to take in redeeming the energy of this word, what I call in this book, the colonizing 'N' word. A word used so negatively. A word that has been deliberately potentized to herald the delivery of insult, wounding, destruction and death, when uttered. After all, Whites have enslaved and killed Blacks in the name of the N word. But like the Surgeon General, a physician, who would come before the public and sound a health alert, I come before you as a Metaphysician to sound a Psychological and Spiritual alert about this word and its potency.

As an Afrikan people we are millions of years old. As we made our footsteps out of Afrika we populated the world. As such, the Medew Netcher have gone forth as a language that has journeyed out of Afrika also. As the Medew Netcher journeyed out of Afrika it became garbled, confused and distorted by its distillation through the English language. The N word(s) has resulted in a concentrated pollutant of darkness and despair which has contributed to the deep psychological scarification that we experience as Afrikan and Afrikan Diaspora. Yet paradoxically, herein lies the greatest Light also.

How is this so? Words have a vibration. Words may vibrate at a higher Spiritual level, a more refined level. When Medew Netcher was vibrating at this higher Spiritual and refined level this contributed to our greatness as an Afrikan people. Likewise, words may vibrate at a lower, coarse, dense and material level. As the Medew Netcher went out into English, - 'words' - were negatively potentized to contribute to our demise as a people.

In the fuller version of my book, Secrets of Race & Consciousness, I dispel the words Negroes, Nigger, and many others that have contributed to our deep psychological wounding; words that we must now understand and overcome. But how will we overcome? Shall we bury the Niger River too and not speak its name? Does not the Niger river have the same Medew Netcher as the N word, N-i-g-e-r

The Golden Sun Egg Uncracked
The Spiritual Meaning of Neggur
Dr Nteri Nelson

or N-i-g-g-e-r? These words have Ancient origin which must be understood. Even though this potency has been used negatively, if the N word did not have this potency it would not have the power to wound. Likewise, this same potency, when used positively, is the power to resurrect and heal. It is this power that must be understood as we look at the journey of the N word as it moved from Medew Netcher, divine speech, and became distillated through the English language.

If we were to find a diamond at the bottom of a dumpster under tons of garbage - *it is still a diamond.* Herein lies the greatest Light to be discovered, a Light that has been hidden, but will be reveled once more. The irresistible pull to give utterance to this word must be understood. After all, Black youth today both kill and greet one another in the name of the N word. There must be a reason and we must understand these reasons. And, once again Kem-unity, we will be duped if we do not look deeply into these matters. To have a half truth is to have a lie. There are two sides to every story and our story must be told in its completeness.

We must look at this bridging that has occurred in language as the Medew Netcher have gone out and what has happened as we crossed over that bridge. We must understand the unification in consciousness that language gives. We must also understand the fragmentation in consciousness that language can likewise give if it is used negatively. We must understand what has happened as we went from 'Kunta Kinte' to 'Toby' and from 'Toby' back again.

The Nu 'N' word in contrast to the colonizing 'N' word, brings us into an understanding of a state of Unitive consciousness and how as an Afrikan people we move from this Unitive State. This was a state of wholeness when we were with the Medew Netcher, when we were with the divine speech of the Gods, when all that we built through the sounding of a 'word' reflected that divinity. As the Medew Netcher moved out we began to experience fragmentation, separativeness, and brokenness in consciousness.

Understanding the N word and the Nu 'N' word is the pathway to understanding the resurrection of ourselves. We cannot get where we need to go using a Eurocentric paradigm that leaves many parts of our story out. We must move within an Afrikan Psychology which will tell the whole story. We cannot tell the story of Humanity's Psychological and Spiritual Journey of Unfolding Consciousness with all the necessary inclusivity unless we are willing to tell the truth about the greatness of the Afrikan Race, the Black Race. Any other story will only tell parts and pieces. As One Human Family we will move from a state of *piece and fragmentation* to a state of *peace and unification* when we see more fully and clearly.

The Golden Sun Egg Uncracked
The Spiritual Meaning of Neggur
Dr Nteri Nelson

Our day of being 'spooked up' is being concluded. Our day of confusion is being concluded. We have been told that there are secrets. But in my books, *The Secrets of Race and Consciousness,* and *Ka Ab Ba Building The Lighted Temple,* one thing we will hopefully come to appreciate is that the *biggest secret* is that there are *no secrets*! All may be revealed to the illumined mind, to one who has a chastened heart, to one who is pure in Spirit. Have we not done the work as a people to have an illumined mind, to have a chastened heart and to be pure in Spirit?

It is time to access the so called secrets that were common place to us, like walking and talking and breathing - before they became the private enterprise for the few. We must get ever so skillful in our treatment of the N word. Knowledge and bridging back from English to Medew Netcher is the way that we will become skillful in resurrecting who we are.

This is a special day and I give praise and appreciation to the initial bold steps taken by the NAACP in redeeming the N word. But we must hold an even greater awareness. In re-claiming our Kemetic Laws, the Law of Rebirth and the Law of Reincarnation, we must understand the knowledge that, *there is no death.* So where there has been a so called 'burial' there must now be a process of redeeming and resurrecting. So let us come together as a Kem-unity to understand the knowledge necessary for this pathway. The Medew Netcher, the Netcherw are being belched up all over this Planet and they are speaking to us. They seek the redemption, the rise, the lift vibratorially that is to be accorded the divine words and speech of the Gods.

▲ Negative Definitions and Meaning of The Colonizing 'N' Word

When we look up these Netcherw, letters or words we are immediately confronted with negative and derogatory definitions and meanings.

Definition: *Merriam-Webster Dictionary.*

Negro - 1. sometimes offensive: a member of the black race distinguished from members of other races by usually inherited physical and physiological characteristics without regard to language or culture; especially: a member of a people belonging to the African branch of the black race. 2. sometimes offensive: a person of Negro descent. Etymology: Spanish or Portuguese, from negro black, from Latin *nigr-, niger.* Date: 1555.

Definition: *American Heritage Dictionary.*

Negro - 1. A member of a major human racial division traditionally distinguished by physical characteristics such as brown to black pigmentation and often tightly curled hair, especially one of various peoples of sub-Saharan African. 2. A person of Negro descent: "Discrimination is a hellhound that gnaws at Negroes in every waking moment of their lives to remind them that the lie of their

inferiority is accepted as truth in the society dominating them" (Martin Luther King, Jr.).
Nigger - n. Offensive. Slang. 1. Used as a disparaging term for a Black person: Used as a disparaging term for a member of any dark-skinned people.

As we dispel the word, Netcher or Name, 'Negroes', we find that the word itself is defined in the dictionary as 'sometimes offensive', something that would seemingly suggest a 'lower material vs. a Higher Spiritual vibration.

▲ Word Vibration and Language as Unification in Consciousness

It is through language that some central unity may be realized. Language may aid this unification in consciousness that we seek in Wsirian/Ausarian resurrection or it may block it. It is in language that an At-One-ing may occur between the Root Races that are running their course on the Planet. This is expressed accordingly: Albert Churchward. *Signs and Symbols of Primordial Man,* p. 227.

> Gesture-signs and ideographic symbols alone preserve the early language in visible figures, and we are unable to get to the roots of all that have been pictured, printed or written, until we can decipher the figures made primarily by the early man. The latest forms of these have to be traced back to the most primary before we can get to know anything of the origins. These are the true radicals of language, without which the philologist

has no final and adequate determinative; and yet these have been left hitherto outside the range of discussion by the Aryan School [read here: Aryan/European consciousness]. But the doctrine is prevalent in current philology, whilst the earlier sign-language has been ignored altogether.

Whenever the ideographic sign of the oldest civilized nations can be compared, evidence of the original unity becomes apparent, and if we take the earliest inhabitants of any part of the World, we find from the skeletons that these were all of the same class-Negroid, just as we find in gesture-language that the further we go back the nearer is our approach towards some central unity. ...To know anything with certitude we must go back the way we came, along the track that only the evolution is free to pursue and explore. We know now that the dumb think, and that man had a gesture-language when he was otherwise dumb.

▲Bridging Between the Language of Medew Netcher and English

We are in an ongoing process of trying to work back from the more primal symbols of the inner language and forward to that which is more exoterically expressed through language. As previously stated, the Netcherw are letters and ideagraphs, the symbols used to give voice to the divine qualities of God. English is that language that Afrikan American and numerous Afrikan Diaspora were forced to learn. In contrast, the Medew Netcher of our Ancient Afrikan Ancestors had become a 'lost language' until the discovery of the Rosetta stone in 1799. This discovery assisted the work of Champolion in the re-translation of a language that had become silent with the destruction and closing of the Ancient mystery schools in Kemet.

English is an outer language that is both spoken and written all over the World, thus it is giving architectural design and arrangement to the world and world affairs. However, it is just a distillate of all other languages that have preceded it. English would suggest itself as the last place to look for derivation on the words, *Negro or Nigger*. Nevertheless, someone said it well when they said, 'If you don't want someone to find something put it right under their nose.' Is it possible to use both the eldest language Medew Netcher and the more recent language English to 'navigate our way Home' again - the Wsir/Ausarian resurrection in consciousness. As restated in the previous quote, 'To know anything with certitude we must go back the way we came, along the track that only the evolution is free to pursue and explore'. Therefore, the following diagram illustrates our movement in going back along the way we came:

Medew Netcher ⟷ English

Let's continue to dispel the name: Negg ur, Negneg ur, Gengen ur. As we look at the consonants, we start by appreciating that each letter or Netcher is a Divine Being, that is:
the 'N' is a divine being
the 'I' or 'E' is a divine being,
the 'G" is a divine being
the 'R' is a divine being
and so on

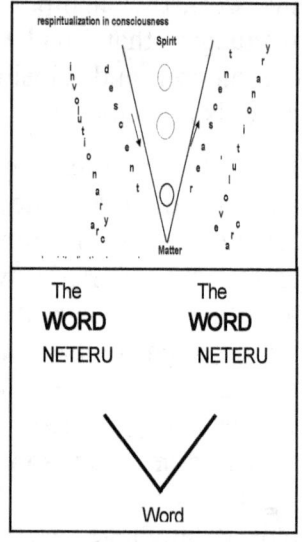

When put together they act as Oracle or Messenger for the Gods. We see pictured in the diagram at right that the Netcherw or WORD has *gone out* in its involutional descent into matter and returns in its evolutionary re-ascent into Spirit. We can see how the Netcherw (letters) in
'N-G-R-I' may move from a positive life promoting and unifying vibration, to a vibration that is destructive, disintegrating and life negating when sounded. In our Afrikan Cosmology of the Goose-goddess who laid the Cosmic Sun Egg words may be seen as having a Positive, Neutral or Negative vibration and meaning in Medew Netcher and English, depending on intent, invocation and circumstance. This is demonstrated in the word list that follows:

The Golden Sun Egg Uncracked
The Spiritual Meaning of Neggur
Dr Nteri Nelson

Mdw Ntr		English		Other
E.A. Wallis Budge. An Egyptian Hieroglyphic Dictionary .V. 1 & II		The American Heritage Dictionary of The English Language		
Neggur the goose-goddess who laid the sun-egg Gengen ur - the Goose-god who laid the Cosmic Egg Neter, Netcher, Netjer, Ntr, Net-ger, N-G-R - God, Divine, or qualities of Divinity Negau - bull, ox, cow (symbols of fertility/ generativity) Neg - bull, bull of bulls Neg - the four horned bull god of heaven Negau - the doorkeeper of the 4th Pylon Neg - to cackle	Negengen - to destroy, to break in pieces Neg,nega - to strike, to smite, to cut off, to cut open, to hew, to slay to crush Neg, nega - to lack, to want, to be short of, to be few in number Negeb - to break, to be destroyed, to come to an end Negebgeb - to break Negeb - a water god Negemgem - to	Negus, Negoos - (King, title Ethiopian Emperors) Negress Negro Green – negre, **Meaning:** Afrikans/Negroes are to the human kingdom what vegetables are to the vegetable kingdom - we blanket the earth, giving life and vitality. Dr Nteri Engender Negotiate Generous Gene Generativity	Denigrate Degenerate Niggardly Nigger Ignorant Indigent English Genuflect Genocide Gentrification Negative Neglect Negation Negro Renege Gun Gang Hung	We find some powerful uses of the N word in the Kikongo language. A short list of Kikongo words and their meaning is given accordingly: Dr Kimbwandende Kia Bunseki Fu-Kiau **Kikongo** Nginga - Seed Dr Nteri seed is synonymous with

66 Afrikan Cosmogenesis & Cosmology of Kemet
The Nu 'N' Word

Negg - to cackle to quack Negaga - to cackle, to quack Nega - cackler Negneg - ur - no meaning listed Negaga - ur - no meaning listed Negit - one of the eight weeping goddesses Negagat - pendent of the breasts of a woman Negait - semen, essence Negnit - a goddess (solar?) who befriended the dead Neges - to overflow Ngesges - to be heaped up full with something, to overflow, overloaded, overflowing	conspire against, to hatch a plot Negen - to cut, to slay Negeh - to be weak, inactive	Genital Genius Integrity Intelligence Integer Ignite Negative Integrate Gynecology 'ing' all action, to be, to do Engineer Dignity Energy English Enlighten King Q(g)ueen Generation Granite (see statues in Kemet, made of) Genuflect Genuine Nzinga – Queen of Angola Gang Genii Magnify Hung (hekau, mantra)		egg Mwene Kongo - King NGIENA - I AM Ngolo - Energy, power, electricity Zinga - Living Ngindu - Psyche Me Mpungu - God Almighty Kinenga - balance Nganga - Masters Ku Kanga – school of initiation N'king-umia-nzingila - Principles of life/living Kalunga - One-who-is-complete-by-self, the all-in-all Yungual

The Golden Sun Egg Uncracked
The Spiritual Meaning of Neggur
Dr Nteri Nelson

					- to burn up
Gengen ur - the Goose-god who laid the Cosmic Egg Gengen - t - a seed or plant used in medicine Gengenu - records, archives, annals Gen - reed, plant, water plants Genur - a god who presides over offerings Gen urit - goddess of offerings Genn - to be gentle or gracious Gen - petitioner, to beseech Gen-t - heap, abundance Genu - a kind of bird, crane Genbut - a man with wooly hair Gemh - sight, glance, look	Gen - to cry out, to beg. Gen - to be weak, helpless, limp Genn - to be weak, helpless, to be paralysed or spellbound Genn - weaknesses, defects, troubles Genf - to revile to abuse Genmu- servants, vassals Genkh - to work Genkha - to be subject to, to toil under orders Gemh - to weep, to mourn				Negus nagast – king Nigiste Nagast - queen, *Historical Dictionary of Ethiopia By David Hamilton Shinn*, p. 220. *(Ethiopia)* Huang – King Columbia Encyclopedia, Sixth Edition Date: 2008 *(China)* Yang di-Pertuan Negara - "He who is made Lord of the State

Gemh - to see, to look, to perceive Gen-t - memorial, record, archive, memorandum				- Malay royalty (Malay) **Ngweny ama - King** *royal title (Swazi)* Ghana - King title 'war chief' *History Corner, The Empire of (Ghana)* Gangga Negara - "a city on the Ganges", the name derived from Gangana gar Kingdom *(Sanskrit)* Gyname - This west African symbol means"

The Golden Sun Egg Uncracked
The Spiritual Meaning of Neggur
Dr Nteri Nelson

					None know the beginning or end of the world except for God.
Kring - Mantra, Hekau (Metu Neter, Sanskrit)					**Royal Names.** *Chinaroad Lowchen.* Konge - King *(Danish)* Koning - King *(Dutch)* Konig - King *(German)* Konnungur - King *(Icelandi)* Kung - King *(Sweedish)*

▲ Let's continue to dispel the word **'N-G-R-I'**:
Take each letter one at a time or in combination with one or more letters and derive its meaning.
Derived letter or Netcher list:
N – out of the waters of Nun, Fount of all possibilities
G – the mouth of the Universal God opens, whose breath stands

R – giving rise to the fire of Ra, and the arising of the ALL seeing Eye of Ra
I – the eye that sees

As stated, the Egg Corresponds to the Eye of Ra. Again, this is expressed accordingly in the following:

> In his birth he says, "I am the babe" born as the connecting link betwixt earth and heaven, and as the one who does not die the second death (ch.42). **He issues from the disc or from the egg. He is pursued by the Herrut-reptile, but, as he says, his egg remains unpierced by the destroyer.**
>
> I come forth and advance and my name is unknown. I am yesterday, and my name is 'Seer of millions of years.' I travel, I travel along the path of Heru the Judge. I am the lord of eternity; I feel and I have power to perceive. I am the lord of the **red crown**. I am the Sun's eye, yea, I am **in my egg, in my egg**. It is granted unto me to live therewith. **I am in the Sun's eye,** when it closeth, and I live by the strength thereof. I come forth and I **shine**; I enter in and I come to life. I am in the **Sun's eye**, my seat is on my throne, and I sit thereon with the eye. I am Heru who pass through millions of years. I have governed my throne and I rule it by the words of my mouth; and whether [I] speak or whether [I] keep silence, **I keep the balance even**. Verily my forms are changed. I am the god Unen, from season unto season; what is mine is with me. **I am the only One born of an only One.**

The Golden Sun Egg Uncracked
The Spiritual Meaning of Neggur
Dr Nteri Nelson

▲ King

We can see the many references to the word 'King' in the preceding short list of words and verse. In the verse, Heru, which is you and I, is the **Sun's eye**, Lord of the red crown, and **King** seated upon the throne which he/she rules as the, only One born of an only One, a Sun -Son/Daughter of God. Heru, is the, *Ka rest* (later called the Christ) within you. The battle that is waged between Heru and his jealous brother Set is for ascendancy to the throne, as King.

In our Afrikan Cosmology of the Goose-goddess who laid the Cosmic Sun Egg we see that –
•On a Higher Spiritual Vibration and turn of the spiral we move within/from a state of wholeness and integrity of the Egg with the invocation of the Netcher or name:

Neggur – The Goose-goddess who laid the sun-egg or

Gengen ur – the Goose-god who laid the Cosmic Sun Egg.

•On a Lower Material Vibration and turn of the spiral we move to a state where the Egg has been weakened, cracked, bound, and diminished with the invocation of the Netcherw or name:

Negengen – To destroy or break in pieces.

Meaning:
In dispelling the word Ne-gen gen we see that it reveals 'reduplication' of the Netcherw or letters and similarity in 'sound' to the names of the Golden Sun God, Negg-ur, Negneg ur, Gengen ur. If we reverse the double 'gen gen'

to 'neg neg, then essentially it is to neg neg 2 times or to're-neg'. Again, we become negengen when we lie as a particulate at the bottom of the glass, a diminished state of consciousness, disconnect from our heavenly origins. Unable, unwilling, to ascend the 7 Arits, as the Neg of Heaven.

▲ Let's dispel the word <u>reneg or renege</u>.
Definition: Thesaurus, Dictionary.
Renege - To go back on, break your word, break a promise. 1. To fail to carry out a promise or commitment. See renegade.

▲ Let's dispel the word **Gengen ur.**
If we look at the reduplication in this word, the double 'gen gen', is essentially to, gen gen 2 times or to're-gen'. Let's dispel this word as in, to <u>regen(erate).</u>
Definition: Thesaurus, Dictionary.
Regen(erate) – To reform spiritually or morally. To form, construct, or create anew, especially in an improved state To give new life or energy to; revitalize.

Meaning Continued:
To come back to the consciousness of the fullness of the One True Self you have always been from the beginningless beginning. It is to return to your stationing in your eternal home while/as you do your work in the outer world. A regeneration of your full identity. Putting

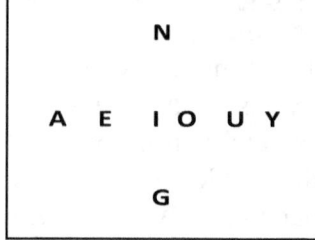

The Golden Sun Egg Uncracked
The Spiritual Meaning of Neggur
Dr Nteri Nelson

the pieces back together again.

▲ Let's return and continue to dispell the word **Neg,** which we have learned is the Bull, Cow and Egg - primal African symbols of life, generativity, virility and fertility. Again, consonants are used to make up a word and convey its primary meaning while vowels may be added/interchanged and lend themselves to facility in pronunciation. This is pictured in the diagram at right.

The word Neg in its higher vibration is invocative of life, birth and knitting/cohering together. At its lower vibration this would become the primal European symbol of the gun. What comes forth from the gun is the bull-et, which brings death, destruction, brokenness/fragmentation.

▲ Let's continue to dispell the word **N-G R-I' by adding the letter K so that we have: N-G K-R-I'**
Take each letter one at a time or in combination with one or more letters and derive its meaning.

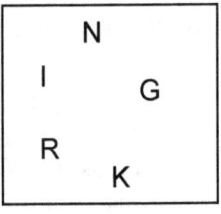

Derived letter or Netcher list:
N – out of the waters of Nun, Fount of all possibilities
G – the mouth of the Universal God opens, whose breath stands
R – giving rise to the fire of Ra, and the arising of the ALL seeing Eye of Ra

I – the eye that sees
K – in all directions of space and time
Meaning:
We see that these same Netcherw when combined and adding the vowel 'e' for ease of pronunciation reveal the words:
R-e-n-e-g-i-n-g King, R-e-i-n-i-n-g King, R-e-n-e-g-a-d-e King, R-e-g-e-n-e-r-a-t-e King

The **R-e-i-n-i-n-g King** is dethroned and becomes.
The **R-e-n-e-g-i-n-g King** less than the fullness of the One True Self.
The **R-e-n-e-g-a-d-e King** abandoning heaven for earth, earth for heaven, one for another, is betwixt and between.
The **R-e-g-e-n-e-r-a-t-i-n-g K-i-n-g** regenerates spiritually as/like the Sun, constructs, creates, anew.

Again, a prayer is made that Wsir/Ausar may,
> 'be saved from the attack made against him "at the crossing." (ch. 135). This indicates that assault on his young divinity is made **as soon as he crosses the line on the west** in his descent. He is then "**the youngling in the egg**" and subject to the Herut attack. Here the dragon lay in wait to devour the young child.

> My nest is not seen, and I have not broken [read here: cracked] my egg. I am lord of millions of years. I have made my nest in the uttermost parts

The Golden Sun Egg Uncracked
The Spiritual Meaning of Neggur
Dr Nteri Nelson

of heaven. I have come down unto the earth of Seb [read here: Geb, Keb]'

▲ Let's dispel the word **Renegade**:
Definition: Dictionary.
Renegade -Spanish renegado, from Medieval Latin renegātus, past participle of *renegāre*, to deny : Latin re-, re- + Latin negāre. To deny. One who rejects a religion, cause, allegiance, or group for another; a deserter. An outlaw; a rebel.

Just what Name is the 44th President Barack Obama really being called in the picture below?

The White and Red Crown* of Kemet and its symbolism becomes distorted into the Crown of the Pope, Santa Claus Hat and the Donald Trump Cap as shown in the pictures below:

---

* See Kemetic Karest mas Celebration & Education by Dr Nteri Nelson, for more information.

76 *Afrikan Cosmogenesis & Cosmology of Kemet*
The Nu 'N' Word

▲ Let's dispell the word **MAGA,** which is acronym for the slogan **M**ake **A**merica **G**reat **A**gain and used by the 45th President Donald Trump.

#16. **Oracle Metaphysical Dis-Spelling Key:** You may un-double a letter's formation, so that one mirrors the other. Example: m would become n n.
Derived word list:

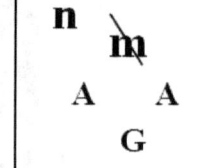

NAGA
Meaning:
This word dispelled reveals the word Naga. Since consonants are interchangeable this word also reveals the words Nega, Nig, Negur – The Great Egg, The Great Neg/Bull of Heaven, The Great Cackler. Again, 'ur' is the word 'Great' in Medu Neter. Symbolic of King, Divine Neter this is the name of Geb, Neb, Lord of the World, Great Being

The Golden Sun Egg Uncracked
The Spiritual Meaning of Neggur
Dr Nteri Nelson

ensouling our Planet Earth. We see here the European attempt to distort, veil and utilize the elevating power of this Name/Neter while simultaneously perverting, potentizing and directing its use to lower and disempower African people

▲ **Looking Further at What the Letter/Netcher 'K' Represents?'**
Not only did the lower vibration of, N-I-G-R and N-G-K-R-I begin to be used but the vibrational energy of the 'K' became distorted in our Afrikan Psyche with the terrorizing that took place in the name of this Netcher under 'KKK' - the Klu Klux Klan. When the energies are invoked in this way they have become inverted and distorted.

The 'K' symbol pictured at right is one of the most powerful symbols in the Ancient Mysteries. When viewed one dimensionally, two K's are seen here turned back to back. However,  you must move within your 1st eye and see this symbol as K's that are rotating, within the sphere, which is the Golden Sun God Egg. If you imagine yourself sitting within this symbol and *spinning* around in all directions like the Jack(s) you perhaps played with as a child - you witness/become the revolving face(s) of the ONE GOD - which sees in all directions. It is a symbol of advanced humanity which is now able to see the 'seeming' other brother's or sister's point of view. ꓘK is the Sema or Smai Tawi symbol of unification that combines the

78 *Afrikan Cosmogenesis & Cosmology of Kemet*
The Nu 'N' Word

Medew Netcher Sema which means union with the symbols for the two lands of Kemet - Papyrus for the North and Lotus flower for the South. In the first Smai Tawi symbol pictured at right, Deities Heru and Set find unity, balance, poise and equanimity within Universal Law.

The Ж or АЖЕ Netcher symbol is likewise the Null, or zero point '0' from which we move from the unmanifest to the manifest. It is the point of arising and moving out it into matter and the point where matter is abstracted back into Spirit. The Smai Tawi symbol is the ancient flooding of the Nile or Hapi River during the Season of Aket. Neteru Hapi are pictured below, making up this same symbol.

This flooding has correspondence with the 'NuN', the arising of the Universal Waters or Life Force, which brings renewal and regeneration. When we practice Shækem RA АЖ E we open ourselves to be as channels for this life giving energy, just as the Nile itself is a life giving channel, flooding its restorative waters. This same symbol, pictured at right is seen carved on the thrones of the Kings of

The Golden Sun Egg Uncracked
The Spiritual Meaning of Neggur
Dr Nteri Nelson

Ancient Kemet. We see King Khafre pictured below:

How Do We Derive This Symbol In The Cosmic Egg?

Recall our Cosmic Egg pictured at right. This is the symbol of the World Egg which then becomes divided in the next three diagrams as follows:

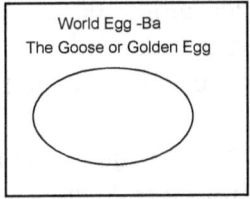

1. The vertical line on the cross of **Spirit-Matter** forming a left and right half of the circle
2. The horizontal line on the cross of **Manifestation** forming an upper and lower circle
3. The arising 4 lines, intersecting each quadrant and forming a crossroad at the center.

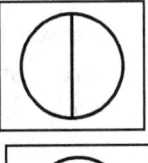
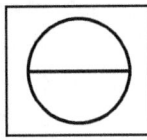

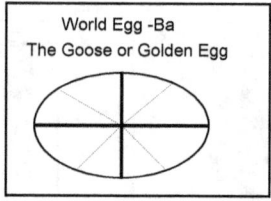

What Do The K's and V's's Represent?

The lines forming the 'V' of the 'K' represent the outgoing footsteps in the Spiritual and Psychological Journey of Unfolding Consciousness in time and space along the involutional and evolutional arc.

• We have been too spooked up to put three K's or KKK together, let alone be in free spin in our consciousness like a Jack.

• We will not restore our sight until we release our fear of KKK.

• Tremendous inversion and distortion has been done to keep us from our Ancient wisdom and what the divine Netcherw (letters) have to reveal.

As we made our footsteps out of Afrika, in the 4 directions of space, we populated the world. As such, the Medew Netcher journeyed as a language out of Afrika also. As the Medew Netcher journeyed out of Afrika it became garbled, confused and distorted by its distillation through the English language. The higher expression of the Nu 'N' word moved from Medew Netcher, divine speech, and

The Golden Sun Egg Uncracked
The Spiritual Meaning of Neggur
Dr Nteri Nelson

became distillated through the English language, as a lower expression and colonizing 'N' word. The resultant concentrated pollutant has contributed to the deep psychological scarification that we experience as Afrikan and Afrikan Diaspora.

In the Afrikan Cosmology of Kemet these outgoing foot steps are symbolized as the foot steps of the Goose, the Goose God, the Neggur, Gengen ur, Negneg ur, *the Ego,* pictured:

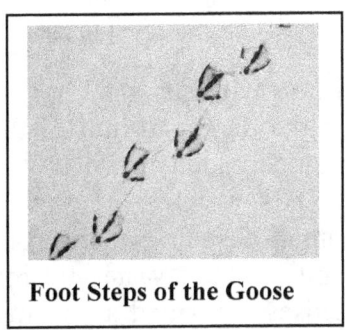

Foot Steps of the Goose

▲ Right of Ascent and Descent of Spirit

1. Spirit has the right to make its deepest descent into matter without abstraction (withdrawal from form) and likewise
2. Spirit has the right to make its greatest ascent (while) in matter (form) without abstraction
3. It is the Law of Vibration in action

We stand as witnesses to a Spiritual law. If we could just bear to see and realize that it has been expressing itself before our very eyes.

▲ What does this mean?

Man is both divine and human. Man has even appeared animal-like and inhuman. It is the Law of Vibration in action. An example will serve to illustrate. Our example takes us aboard a slave ship where we may look at the condition of both the enslaved and captain (enslaver) upon the slave ship. To see the demonstration of the law that Spirit reaches its lowest descent into matter without abstraction – we view first the condition of the one enslaved.

The enslaved lays with shackled hands and feet for weeks now in the darkened hull of the slave ship. His muscles are abraded down to bone which is now exposed. His wounds are raw and infested. Death and human despair are all around him. The stench of vomit, human waste and rotting corpses assaults his senses. Appalled as we may be by this sight, we see that from behind the eyes of this man is *Spirit* – and that – Spirit has the right to find its way into the lowliest material condition without abstraction or death of the form of this man. Even though he cries out to death for release from his agony and suffering, he is living through these conditions.

Next –
We likewise view the captain (enslaver) above on deck the slave ship. The sun is upon the captain's face. Yet he is obsessed and consumed by thoughts of greed and lust. He murders with little or no

The Golden Sun Egg Uncracked
The Spiritual Meaning of Neggur
Dr Nteri Nelson

provocation anyone who thwarts his mission, whether enslaved or crewman. He passes long days on the ship with the sport of slave torture and humiliation. At night he comforts himself with the degradation and rape of enslaved women. Again we see in this man also that *Spirit* has the right of descent into matter without abstraction. Death does not come just because Spirit indwells in the vilest of mental, emotional and physical conditions. Even though in gloating arrogance he taunts death itself, he is living through these conditions.

The Ages of Light followed by the Ages of Dark must be seen as impersonal as the light of day that is followed by the dark cover of night. These cycles contribute to the rise and fall of great civilizations in the ongoing Spiritual journey of man and woman. The optimal, supernal heights are followed by the most debased cycles of debauchery. This is a hard saying. In man's inhumanity to man there has been great injustice.
•So, as we have stood as witnesses to the low in the descent.
•So we will stand in witness to the greatness of re-ascent.

Marcus Garvey expresses this according to: Dr. Tony Martin, *The Ideological and Organizational Struggles of Marcus Garvey.*

> Garveyism decreed that the attainment of its ultimate goals was inevitable, the goals in this case being the resurgence of the Black Race: "In

the cycle of things he lost his position, but the same cycle will take him back to where he was once.

- We will walk once again upon the Earth as Gods
- When Spirit asserts its right to its highest ascent in woman and man
- After much rehearsal in the 7 planes of consciousness along its descent down
- Through the planes of the Tree of Life
- Thus does each Prodigal Sun - Son/Daughter
- Ultimately return Home
- Having gained the entire
- Conscious experience of Spirit
- At every level of its immersion into matter and
- Matter in its re-ascent into pure Spirit
- Every vile and glorious station
- Back to Omniscient consciousness, Wsir/Ausarian Consciousness
- The Spiritual Journey is from God to God
- As you bring your consciousness back
- Into the awareness of the All
- The Amen in The Tree of Life
- You are set back to Ground '0'
- This re-absorption takes place through meditation
- And living in accord
- With the Universal Laws of Maat
- Man finds himself once again
- Polarized in the ONE
- The first sphere of the Tree of Life
- A King upon the thrown
- As the One of Wsir/Ausar Ba
- You are able to draw from The Fount Of All Possibility

The Golden Sun Egg Uncracked
The Spiritual Meaning of Neggur
Dr Nteri Nelson

- All that is needed to work co-creatively
- In the great Divine Plan.
- This Soul awareness attunes you to the source
- Of Omnipotence, Omnipresence, and Omniscience

Meaning Continued: The word **N-G-K-R-I** is an ancient hekau or mantra (word of power) **'K-r-i-n-g'**. This ancient mantra is invocative of power and is to be sounded oracly and circularly as indicated by the diagrams at right. Remember, each letter is a Netcher, a divine quality of God, and a living being. When combined and put in a circle they become a mouthpiece through which God speaks. So God is speaking through the 'N' 'G' 'K' 'R' 'I' or K' 'R' 'I' 'N' 'G'. It is about the intention during 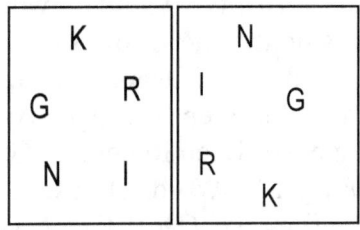 meditation that guides what is manifested in the use of this Medew Netcher. It is important, especially for our youth of today, when sounding this word of power to do so by enunciating the 'N' first by putting the tongue at the roof of the mouth and sounding the rest of the word oracly and circularly as if one continuous sound as in the following:

N-G K-R-I N-G K-R-I N-G K-R-I N-G K-R-I N-G K-R-I N-G K-R-I N-G K-R-I N-G K-R-I-N-G

86 *Afrikan Cosmogenesis & Cosmology of Kemet*
The Nu 'N' Word

Sound the following Hekau with the highest vibratory intention circularly and oracaly, visualizing the color Green while doing healing work so that you may be as One with/as Wsir/Ausar, pictured at right, the Green God of Life and Fertility. We are going GREEN as a Humanity.

▲ Let's Dispell the word **Green:**
Derived word list:
Negre
Meaning:

Afrikans/NGRE(I) are to the human kingdom what vegetables are to the vegetable kingdom – We blanket the earth, giving life, fertility, virility, vitality while harnessing the energy of/as the Sun – Son/Daughter.

▲ **In Meditation Deep, affirm:**
• I Have Not Been Negengen As An Afrikan
• I Have Not Been Reneging, Going Back On, Breaking My Word, Breaking My Promise, Nor Failing To Carry Out My Promise, My Commitment
• I Have Not Been Negengen, Renegade, Failing To Come Back To The Consciousness Of The Fullness Of The One True Self That I Have Always Been From The Beginningless Beginning.
• I Have Not Been Negengen, Renegade From My Stationing In My Eternal Home While/As I do My Work In The Outer World.
• I Have Not Been Negengen Causing Us To suffer A Brokenness In Consciousness Of

The Golden Sun Egg Uncracked
The Spiritual Meaning of Neggur
Dr Nteri Nelson

Who We Are As Sun-Sons/Daughters Of GOD
• I Have Not Been Reneging On My Full Identity Or I.D, Causing My Continued Dethroning As King/Queen.
• I Am The Gengen ur, Great Regenerating Life Sun
• I Re-Gain Ascendency To The Throne Within By Holding The Forces In-Balance
• I AM The Reining King, 'N-G K-R-I' On My Throne, The Fullness Of The One True Self That I AM And Have Always Been From The Beginingless Beginning

▲ The Spiritual Implications Of The Perfect Storm/Where Are We Today?

In the diagram below, the vertex in the letter 'V' illustrates how Spirit has made its deepest descent into matter. As greater descent is reached in the involutionary time cycle, man's consciousness has become more materialized. Along the way humanity has gradually lost sight of the interconnecting webworm and interdependence between all kingdoms of life. Individualism reigns as man and woman have come to see themselves as a self separated from all other 'selves'. Today humanity sits perched within the vertex of the 'V' having reached the greatest point of materialization and darkness in consciousness. It is now well into its struggle to start turning the corner in the vertex, thus in its arduous uphill climb toward the re-spiritualization in consciousness. The Spiritual

88 Afrikan Cosmogenesis & Cosmology of Kemet The Nu 'N' Word

Waters are rising and meet with the contending Material forces. *The Spiritual Tides and the Material Tides Clash.*

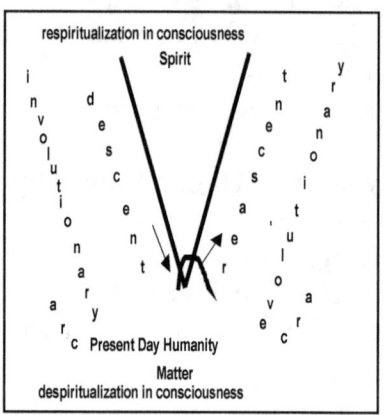

▲ The Egg of Consciousness
Ka Ab Ba and The 3 primary Egoic states of Consciousness

Our Afrikan Ancestors were Masters in: a) the Science of Mind, Body and Soul b) developing divine qualities which they called the Netcher or Netcherw and c) detailing the anatomy of the Soul, its Journey, and how to fulfill ones life purpose. The 3 primary Egoic States in Consciousness may be observed as follows:

1. Consciousness may remain Unitive.
2. Consciousness may become Dualized and Reconciliative/Combative.
3. Consciousness may become Separative or Particularized into many.

The Golden Sun Egg Uncracked
The Spiritual Meaning of Neggur
Dr Nteri Nelson

▲ Return to KaAbBa Consciousness

How we perceive the inner and outer World depends upon which of these 3 primary Egoic states we find ourselves identified with. The qualities each expresses is shown in the following diagram:

When we come full circle, putting the pieces back together again, we are conscious and affirm:
- I know the One in the Many.
- I know the One and the same Self in all the seeming self appearances.
- I know simultaneous - one-at-a-time-ness, in-between-ness-and All-at-once-ness.

The Egg As Symbol of Planetary and Human Consciousness

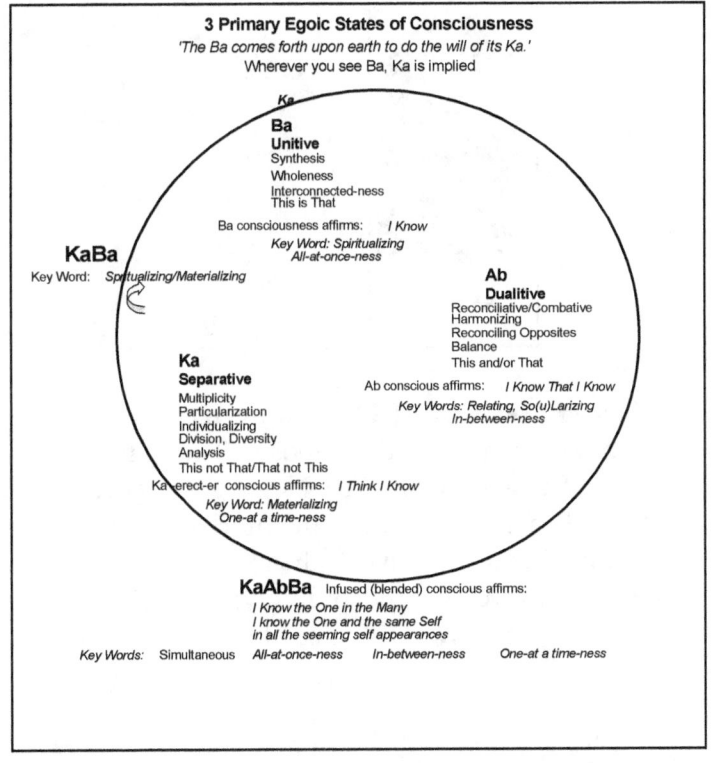

90 *Afrikan Cosmogenesis & Cosmology of Kemet*
The Nu 'N' Word

▲ The Vertex In The V Understanding What Time It Is

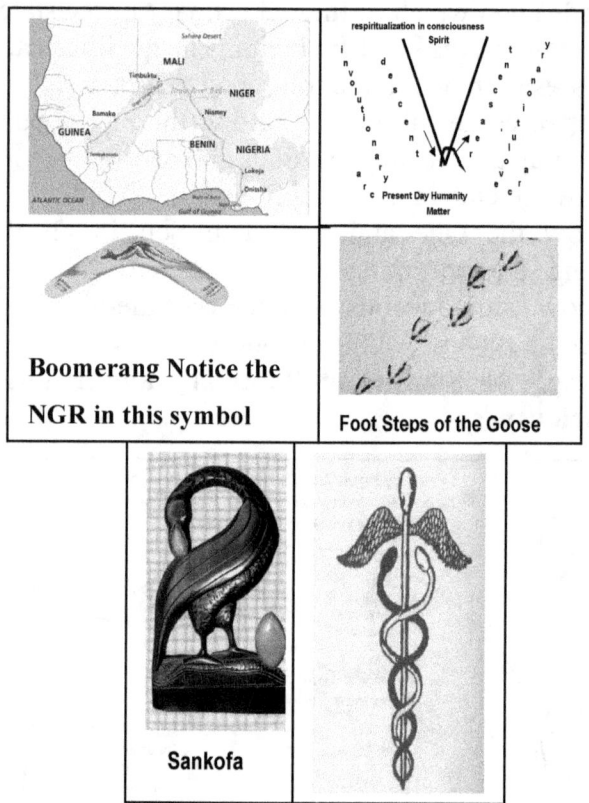

| Boomerang Notice the NGR in this symbol | Foot Steps of the Goose |

Sankofa

▲ Sacred Meaning of The Caduceus

We have seen that the Goose, The Great Cackler Neggur, Gengen ur, Negneg ur, 'goes out' and begins a cycle of time. All the symbols pictured above indicate 'a return'. This is expressed accordingly: Geoffrey Barborka. *The Divine Plan,* p. 218.

The Golden Sun Egg Uncracked
The Spiritual Meaning of Neggur
Dr Nteri Nelson

The tree of Life and Being, the Rod of the caduceus grows from and descends at every Beginning (every new manvantara) from the two dark wings of the Swan Hansa (also read here: Hamsa/Kamsa) of Life. The two Serpents, the ever-living and its illusion (Spirit and matter) whose two heads grow from the one head between the wings, descends along the trunk, interrelated in close embrace. The two tails join on earth (the manifested Universe) into one and this is the great illusion, O Lanoo!

The Caduceus or Kaduceus is pictured at right: Here the caduceus symbolizes all that is needed and divinely intended. When actualized it is the fullest measure of the divine image and likeness of God reflected in matter. It is how the Ka - Spririt succeeds along its descent and re-ascent of the Tree of Life. Our Afrikan Ancestors studied nature all around them.

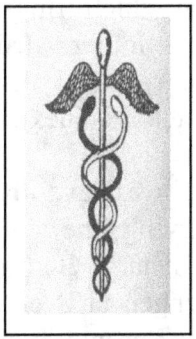

The serpent is a symbol of wisdom, healing and medicine. If we were bitten by a snake, nature teaches us that we have 3 simple options.
1. We may lay there and die. *Not an option*
2. We may wait for someone to come by and suck the poison out of us. *Not an option*
3. We may find the antidote of the serpent and take this medicine. *Aha*

Afrikan Cosmogenesis & Cosmology of Kemet
The Nu 'N' Word

Our antidote is to rid ourselves from that which has poisoned us with its toxin. If we lie dying from the snake bite of the colonizing 'N' word, is there anything medicinal and serpentine in embracing the Nu'N' Word, Neggur, Gengen ur, Negneg ur, in our journey? Are our youth, seemingly misquided in the use of the N word or tapping into an ancient harmonic in search of healing.

As we embrace the Nu'N' Word we see the probable distortions of ancient harmonics and retrace with our footsteps, a path deep within our Afrikan Cosmology and Cosmogenesis. We (particularly our youth) thereby reconnect ourselves to that which 'rings true' to our story, our healing and our Mother Afrika. Through this reconnection we see revealed that the resurrection of the Medew Netcher is inextricably linked with our own.

Do we have the courage to move beyond, just burying the colonizing N word? After all, the Planetary God of our Earth is named, Neggur, Gengen ur, Negneg ur. He is called Geb, the Great Cackler and he is the Father of Wsir/Ausar, who is Lord of the World. Can we go back through the 'Port of the Geese' – through which we came in the Portuguese slave trade and the 'Door of No Return' through which we came to return and remember our ancient teachings? Can we ungarble what has been garbled and undistort that which has been distorted.

The Golden Sun Egg Uncracked
The Spiritual Meaning of Neggur

Dr Nteri Nelson

▲ Can We Remember?
Geese Facts

Next fall when you see geese heading south for the winter... flying along in V formation...you might consider what science has discovered as to why they fly that way:

As each bird flaps its wings, it creates an uplift for the bird immediately following. By flying in V formation, the whole flock adds at least 71% greater flying range, than if each bird flew on its own.

People who share a common direction and sense of community can get where they are going more quickly and easily because they are traveling on the thrust of one another.

When a goose falls out of formation, it suddenly feels the drag and resistance of trying to go it alone... and quickly gets back into formation to take advantage of the lifting power of the bird in front. If we have as much sense as a goose, we will stay in formation with those who are headed the same way we are.

When the head goose gets tired it rotates back in the wing and another goose flies point. It is sensible to take turns doing demanding jobs...with people or with geese flying south.

Geese honk from behind to encourage those up front to keep up their speed. What do we say when we honk from behind?

Finally...and this is important...when a goose gets sick or is wounded by gunshots, and falls out of formation, two other geese fall out with that goose and follow it down to lend help and protection. They stay with the fallen goose until it is able to fly or until it dies, and only then do they launch out on their own, or with another formation to catch up with their group.

If we have the sense of a goose, we will stand by each other like that.

Author Unknown

The Golden Sun Egg Uncracked
The Spiritual Meaning of Neggur
Dr Nteri Nelson

African Cosmology, African Centered Education
The Psychological & Spiritual Journey
of Unfolding Consciousness
Metaphysics and Mysteries

KaAbBa

Kemet (also spelled Kmt, Kamit) is land within the Ancient Nile Valley Civilization in Africa and its people were called the Kemetians. This land and its people would later be re-named Egypt and Egyptians respectively, by the Greeks. These Kemites, our African Ancestors, used picture images or ideographs from nature all around them to communicate ideas, which is the language they called MTU NTR, MTW NTR, METU NETER or MEDU NETER. These symbols were later re-named Hieroglyphics by the Greeks.

The Medu Neter, Ka Ab Ba, are pictured below.

Ka   **Ab**   **Ba**

Our African Ancestors were Masters in the 'Science of the Soul' and 'Journey of the Soul'. They were Master Psychologists, Spiritual Practitioners, Metaphysicians or what may be called here, Kemeticians. They have given us these 3 primary Medu Neter for:
1. Understanding the Spiritual and Physical Anatomy of Man., Woman and Cosmos
2. Unlocking the Psychological and Spiritual Journey in Unfolding Consciousness
3. Unfettering the Soul from that which would threaten to impede it in its Journey

Why did our African Ancestors focus within these 3 Primary Medu Neter - *Ka Ab Ba***?**
To answer this question the following analogy may best serve. When we 'click onto' an icon on our Windows computer screen, whole documents are opened up and a panorama of information is revealed to our poised and awaiting mind or mental field. By analogy, the 3 primary Medu Neter are like these icons which were used by our Kemetic Ancestors. As we 'click' in turn onto the Medu Neter *Ka, Ab,* and *Ba,* the Psychological and Spiritual Journey in Unfolding Consciousness is revealed. These ideographs or pictures are the 'Divine idea and speech' which open our 1st eye and aid us to glimpse the Whole Moving Geometry within in the Mind of God. Thus, as the Journey

unfolds, we are able to see the changing states in our consciousness which lead to changing states in our physical World.

On the Psycho/Spiritual Journey in Unfolding Consciousness what are you as the Sun-Son/Daughter becoming fully conscious of?

For the Kemetians Ka means Spirit. In the Metaphysical Keys that follow, you will see that, Ka – Spirit, takes of the substance of ITSELF to see ITSELF in form. Ka – Spirit, takes of the substance of ITSELF to have consciousness in form. Ka – Spirit, takes of the substance of ITSELF and begins to differentiate itself in/as Spirit-matter. This is one of the many Divine paradoxes. As much as Spirit is UNLIMITED and UNCONDITIONED it asserts its right to limit itself in form or matter in order to gain conscious experience of ITSELF. In various grades of material form, IT – Ka, sees ITSELF. It is in *the seeing of ITSELF* that consciousness is born. Thus we are made Divine and human, Spiritual and material. For the Kemetians Ba means Soul and Soul is consciousness. Therefore, Ba is an individualization of Spirit. We are told that Ka - Spirit precedes Ba Soul. This is expressed in the following accordingly: Alvin Boyd Kuhn, *The Lost Light*, p. 588.

> "The Ba comes forth upon earth to do the will of its Ka.

This is derived from the Ritual Text of the *Prt Em Hru* which is expressed accordingly: E.A. Wallis Budge. *The Egyptian Book of the Dead*, p. 359.

> The souls come forth to do the will of their Ka's and the soul of Ausar Ani cometh forth to do the will of his Ka.

The Soul-Ba comes forth upon the Earth to do the will of its Spirit-Ka.

For the Kemetians Ab symbolizes the human heart. The heart is the seat of the Soul, the conscience and growing Self conscious identity. The Ab Soul is the conscious experience of how Spirit and Matter are relating. As man's consciousness develops, he must also develop a 'conscience'. This is Heru or the Karest/Christ principle within you that guides you to be and act in accord with the Universal Law of Right Relationship. Through the relating aspect of Ab, the 'seeming' duality between Spirit-Matter with its myriad objective forms in play and display as Ba Ka are seen as ONE. Thus through Ab Soul consciousness the same One True Self is seen in every other Self.

This is expressed in the diagram at right. On our Psycho Spiritual Journey in Unfolding Consciousness as Heru - sphere 6 in the Tree of Life, we make our descent into material life conditions. As Heru we are Sun-Son/Daughter. On our return journey, we make our hard, arduous climb of re-ascent Home again, into the Spiritual

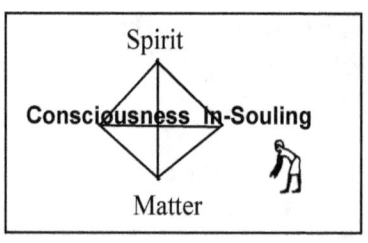

realms. You are becoming fully conscious of the perfect relationship between Father and Mother and Spirit and Matter. To become fully conscious is to live the consciousness of Ausar Ba - that we are made in the Image and Likeness of God and All SELVES are but the ONE True Indivisible SELF.

How does the Creator Create?
The Creator does not go to Home Depot, The Creator creates by taking from the sub-stance of Itself.

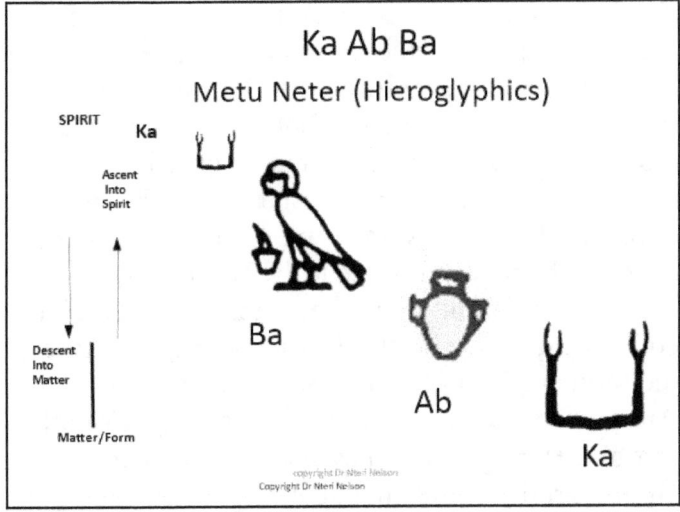

In referring to the diagram above we see that:
Ka is Spirit, represented by the smaller upstretched arms, at the top left of the diagram. Ka, Spirit takes of the substance of Itself to see Itself in form, represented by the larger upstretched arms at the

bottom right of the diagram. This is the physicalizing or form making aspect of Ka. Thus, Ka is called Double in both Its Spiritualizing and Physicalizing aspects. On the lefthand side in this diagram, we see the Spirit-Matter Continuum indicated by the arrows, which gives innerstanding on the Law of Vibration (described earlier). That is, All is Spirit. Spirit is Matter at its lower level of vibration and Matter is Spirit at its higher level of vibration. Thus Ka as Spirit vibrates at levels more Spiritual and refined and levels more Material, coarse and dense.

Ka, Spirit does not just seek to see Itself in form. Ka, Spirit takes of the substance of Itself to have consciousness in form(s) It indwells. This is represented by Ab, the symbol of the heart and the seat of conscience and growing Soul Consciousness. As consciousness or Ab grows, it becomes Ba in fullest measure of consciousness (as noted in the reversal of the Mdw Ntr letters, Ab and Ba). It is important to note here that Ka Ab Ba have correspondence with the Divine Trinity of Auset - the Mother, Heru - the Sun-Son/Daughter and
Ausar - the Father within us, respectively. From left to right, Heru, Ausar and Auset are pictured, as the Divine Trinity, on the next page:

The Golden Sun Egg Uncracked
The Spiritual Meaning of Neggur
Dr Nteri Nelson

Ab becoming Ba is the fullest Self Realization as the One True Self, in Consciousness. The Kemites teach that one can then affirm: Inuk Ausar, Inuk Auset. I am Ausar, I am Auset. My Father, my Mother and I are One. Christianity would later affirm this state in Consciousness as: My Father and I are One.

Oracle Metaphysical Dis-Spelling Keys

> **Metaphysical Keys to:**
> **Oracle Metaphysical Dis-Spelling Keys**

In using the Metaphysical Dis-Spelling Keys along with many other Metaphysical Keys to the Tree of Life we will attempt to break the 'spell of illusion' in our re-ascent up the Tree of Life.

 # 1. Oracle Metaphysical Dis-Spelling Key:
Put letters of word or words together in a circle, like a serpent putting its tail in its mouth. Coming full Circle.

#2. Oracle Metaphysical Dis-Spelling Key:
Read letters, putting together words, going forwards, backwards and in zig-zag patterns.

#3. Oracle Metaphysical Dis-Spelling Key:
You may crossover in order to use a letter more than once. Place re-used letter in parenthesis ( ).

#4. Oracle Metaphysical Dis-Spelling Key:
You may add a letter to complete a word. Place added letter in parenthesis ( ).

#5. Oracle Metaphysical Dis-Spelling Key:
Letter substitution-you may substitute a letter. Place substituted letter in parenthesis ( ).

#6. Oracle Metaphysical Dis-Spelling Key:
Make a list of derived words. Try to make the longest continuous unbroken word or string of words.

#7. Oracle Metaphysical Dis-Spelling Key:

The Golden Sun Egg Uncracked
The Spiritual Meaning of Neggur
Dr Nteri Nelson

Look up definition (dictionary, glossary, reference texts, etc.)

#8. Oracle Metaphysical Dis-Spelling Key: Meaning. See the relationship and oracle or story of the Neteru - Put word list together to tell a story.

#9. Oracle Metaphysical Dis-Spelling Key: Take each letter one at a time or in combination with one or more letters and derive its meaning.

#10. Oracle Metaphysical Dis-Spelling Key: Letter replacement. Here we have replaced the 'k' which had been substituted by the letter 'c.'

#11. Oracle Metaphysical Dis-Spelling Key: What does the word sound like? Say the word out loud and then silently in a meditative state.

#12. Oracle Metaphysical Dispelling Key: Take out duplication of letters so that each letter appears only once.

#13. Oracle Metaphysical Dis-Spelling Key: You may abrade a letter so that it is changed to another letter as in 'h' to 'n'. Notice the loping off of the top of the 'h' to make 'n'.

Definition: Dictionary

Abrade - 1. To wear down or rub away by friction; erode. See synonyms at chafe. 2. To make weary through constant irritation; wear down spiritually. (Latin abradere, to scrape of: ab-, away.

#14. **Oracle Metaphysical Dis-Spelling Key:**
You may add the letter T which symbolizes the Ankh or Tau cross of Spirit and Matter.

#15. **Oracle Metaphysical Dis-Spelling Key:**
You may combine two or more words as one word.

#16. **Oracle Metaphysical Dis-Spelling Key:** You may un-double a letter's formation, so that one mirrors the other. Example: m would become n n.

Select Bibliography & Suggested Reading List

Adler, Vera Stanley. *The Initiation of The World*. York Beach, ME: Samuel Weiser, 1972.

African World History Project. Los Angeles, CA: Association for the Study of Classical African Civilizations, 2002.

Amen, Ra Un Nefer. *Metu Neter, V.I & II*. Bronx, NY: Khamit Corp., 1990.

Arquelles, Jose. *The Mayan Factor*. Santa Fe, New Mexico: Bear & Company, 1987.

Arquelles, Jose. *The Surfers of the Zuvuya*. Santa Fe, New Mexico: Bear & Company, 1989.

Ashby, Dr. Muata. *The Ausarian Resurrection*. Miami, FL: Cruzian Mystic Books, 1995.

Barborka, Geofrey. *The Divine Plan*. London, England: Theosophical Publishing House, 1964.

Ben-Jochannan, Yosef. *Black Man of The Nile and His Family*. Baltimore, MD: Black Classic Press, 1989.

Blavatsky, H.P. (Scribe). *Isis Unveiled, V.I & II*. Pasadena, CA: Theosophical University Press, 1988.

Blavatsky, H.P. (Scribe). *Secret Doctrine, V.I & II*. Theosophical University Press, 1988.

Blavatsky, H.P. *Theosophical Glossary*. Los Angeles, CA: Theosophy Company, 1990.

Bocock Robert. *Freud and Modern Society*. New York, NY: Holmes & Meier, 1978.

Browder, Anthony. *Nile Valley Civilization*. Washington, DC: Institute of Karmic Guidance, 1992.

Budge, E. A. Wallis. *Amulets and Superstitions*. New York, NY: Dover Publications, 1978.

Budge, E. A. Wallis *Prt Em Hru. The Book of Coming Forth By Day*. (Egyptian Book of the Dead). New York, NY: Dover Publications, 1967.

Budge, E. A. Wallis. *Osiris: The Egyptian Religion of Resurrection*. New Hyde Park, NY: University Books, 1961.

Budge, E. A. Wallis. *An Egyipan Hieroglyphic Dictionary, V.I & II*. New York, NY: Dover Publications, 1978.

Budge, E. A. Wallis. *The God of The Egyptians, V.I & II.* New York, NY: Dover Publications, 1969.

Budge, E. A. Wallis *The Egyptian Heaven & Hell.* Chicago and La Salle, Illinois: Open Court Publishing, 1905.

Burgoyne, Thomas. *The Light of Egypt. The Science of the Soul and the Stars. V.I & II.* Santa Fe, NM: Sun Publishing, 1980.

Churchward, Albert. *Signs and Symbols of Primordial Man.* Brooklyn, NY: A & B Books, 1903.

Churchward, Albert. *Origin and Evolution of the Human Race.* London: George Allen & Unwin LTD. 1921.

Churchward, Albert. *Origin and Evolution of Primitive Man.* London: George Allen & Company, 1912.

Churchward, Albert. *The Arcana of Freemasonry.* London: George Allen & Unwin LTD, 1922.

De Lubicz, Isha Schwaller. *Her-Bak: Egyptian Initiate.* Rochester, VT: Inner Traditions International, 1967.

De Lubicz, Isha Schwaller. *The Opening of The Way.* New York, NY: Inner Traditions International, 1981.

Diop, Cheikh Anta. *African Origin of Civilization: Myth or Reality.* Chicago, IL: Lawrence Hill Books, 1974.

Diop, Cheikh Anta. *Civilization or Barbarism.* Brooklyn, NY: Lawrence Hill Books, 1991.

Gardiner, Sir Alan. *Egyptian Grammar Study of Hieroglyphics.* United Kingdom: University Press, 1927.

Hall, Manly P. *Freemasonry of the Ancient Egyptians.* Los Angeles, CA: Philosophical Research Society, 1965.

Heindel, Max. *The Rosicrucian Cosmo-Conception.* Oceanside, CA: Rosicrucian Fellowship, 1988.

Hassan-El, Kashif Malik. The Wilie Lynch Letter and The Making of a Slave. Chicago: Lushena Books. 1712, 1999.

Hurtak. J. J. The Book of Knowledge: The Keys of Enoch. Los Gatos, CA: Academy for Future Science, 1973.

Jackson, John. *Introduction to African Civilizations.* Secausus, NJ: Citadel Press, 1970.

Jackson, John. *Man, God and Civilization.* Secausus, NJ: Citadel Press, 1972.

James, George, G. M.. *Stolen Legacy.* San Francisco CA: Julian Richardson Assoc.1954, 1985. Karenga,. Dr. Malauana. *The 7 Principles of Kwaanza.* Los Angeles, CA: University of Sankore Press, 1988.

The Golden Sun Egg Uncracked
The Spiritual Meaning of Neggur
Dr Nteri Nelson

Krummenaker, Daniel. *Where Were Atlantis And Lemuria?*
Kuhn, Alvin Boyd. *The Lost Light.* Henry Holt & Company,1931.
Lawlor, Robert. *Voices of The First Day.* Rochester, Vermont: Inner Traditions International, Ltd., 1991.
Ligon, A. Black Knostic Study Teachings of Dr. Ligon. (Private Group Study).
LEVI. *Aquarian Gospel of Jesus The Christ.* Marina Del Rey, CA: DeVorss & Co, 1982.
Mackenzie, Donald.*Egyptian Myths and Legends.* Avenel, NJ: Random House Value, 1980.
Massey, Gerald. *Ancient Egypt, The Light of The World V.I & II.* Baltimore, MD: Black Classic Press, 1992.
Massey, Gerald. *A Book of the Beginnings. V.I & II.* Secaucus, NJ: University Books, 1974.
Mead, G.R.S. *Thrice Greatest Hermes.* York Beach, ME: Samuel Weiser, 2001.
Martin, Tony. *Marcus Garvey.* Dover, MA: The Majority Press, 1986.
National Council For Geocosmic Research, 93rd edition.
Nelson, Terri Nelson. *Secrets of Race & Consciousness.* Mattapan, MA: Academy Kemetic Education, 2000.
Nelson, Terri Nelson. *KaAbBa Building The Lighted Temple.* Mattapan, MA: Academy Kemetic Education, 2000.
Nelson, Terri Nelson. *On The Way To Finding Your Soulmate.* Mattapan, MA: Academy Kemetic Education, 1996.
Parfitt, Will. *The Living Qabalah.* Longmead: Element Books, 1988.
Ponce, Charles. *Kabbalah.* Wheaton, IL: The Theosophical Publishing House, 1973.
Regardie, Israel. *The Tree of Life.* York Beach, ME: Samuel Weiser, 1972.
Robbins, Michael. *Infinitizing of Selfhood.* Mariposa, CA: University of The Seven Rays, 1997.
Robbins, Michael.*Tapestry of the Gods. V.I & II.* Jersey City Heights, NJ: University of The Seven Rays, 1988.
Rogers J.A. 100 *Amazing Facts About the Negro.*Helga M. Rogers, St. Petersburg, FL: 1957.
Satguru Sivaya Subramuniyaswami. *Lemurian Scrolls.* India: Himalayan Academy, 1998.
Three Initiates. *The Kybalion, Hermetic Philosophy* Chicago, IL: Yogi Publication Society, 1940.

Afrikan Cosmogenesis & Cosmology of Kemet
The Nu 'N' Word

Tyberb, Judith. *Sanskrit Keys to the Wisdom Religion.* San Diego, CA: Point Loma, 1976.

Tibetan (scribe, A. Bailey). Twenty-Four Books of Esoteric Philosophy, CD-ROM, New York: Lucis Publishing Company, 1998.

Tibetan (scribe, A. Bailey). *Cosmic Fire. Esoteric Astrology. Esoteric Psychology, V.I & II.*

Rays And Initiations. Initiations Human and Solar. See 24 Books as reference source.

Westcott, William Wynn. *Collectanea Hermetica.* York Beach, ME: Samuel Weiser, 1998.

Williams, Chacellor. *The Destruction of Black Civilization.* Chicago, IL: Third World Press, 1987. Wilson, Hilary. *Understanding Hieroglyphs.* Barnes & Noble, Inc. New York, NY:B & N,1993.

The American Heritage Dictionary of The English Language. 3rd Edition. Boston, MA: Houghton Miflon 1992.

Microsoft Word Program. *Thesaurus.* 2003.

www.ingramcontent.com/pod-product-compliance
Lightning Source LLC
Chambersburg PA
CBHW050602300426
44112CB00013B/2029